About Math Connection:

Welcome to Rainbow Bridge Publishing's Connection series. Math Connection provides students with focused practice to help reinforce and develop math skills in all area  National Council of Teachers of Mathematic th-grade students. These include numeration four-digit addition and subtraction, probability, measurement, shapes, graphing, time, money values, word problems, fractions, multiplication, and division. Exercises are grade-level appropriate with clear examples and instructions on each page to guide the lesson; they also feature a variety of activities to help students develop their ability to work with numbers.

Written by Carolyn Chapman
Illustrated by Amanda Sorensen
© 2003 Rainbow Bridge Publishing

ISBN: 1-93221-016-4

Math Connection— Grade 4
Table of Contents

Facts Review: Addition

Add.

1.	2 + 2	4 + 3	9 + 8	6 + 7	10 + 4	6 + 5	11 + 4	3 + 8
2.	5 + 8	1 + 7	8 + 2	1 + 1	7 + 7	11 + 7	2 + 1	8 + 1
3.	7 + 9	4 + 6	1 + 0	11 + 1	2 + 7	10 + 5	8 + 4	9 + 9
4.	11 + 6	8 + 2	10 + 7	2 + 3	4 + 8	6 + 2	3 + 3	1 + 9
5.	0 + 7	9 + 1	4 + 4	3 + 6	2 + 9	12 + 0	6 + 8	3 + 1
6.	1 + 2	11 + 8	5 + 5	12 + 7	10 + 8	8 + 6	12 + 4	8 + 8
7.	0 + 2	4 + 9	5 + 7	7 + 3	9 + 5	10 + 6	7 + 4	11 + 6
8.	11 + 5	6 + 3	9 + 6	7 + 9	3 + 0	8 + 4	1 + 9	6 + 4
9.	4 + 2	11 + 2	4 + 5	6 + 6	12 + 8	9 + 3	8 + 6	12 + 2
10.	9 + 0	6 + 3	6 + 1	12 + 9	2 + 5	7 + 8	10 + 9	3 + 4

5

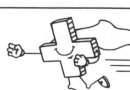

Facts Review: Addition

Add.

1.	7 + 4	8 + 0	1 + 3	6 + 7	2 + 3	8 + 4	8 + 7	2 + 7
2.	12 + 3	2 + 2	6 + 9	5 + 2	10 + 3	11 + 5	5 + 2	5 + 5
3.	0 + 3	5 + 4	4 + 0	6 + 4	12 + 2	6 + 6	9 + 0	4 + 8
4.	3 + 4	0 + 7	9 + 9	1 + 2	12 + 8	8 + 6	2 + 7	7 + 3
5.	6 + 5	4 + 1	2 + 9	10 + 1	3 + 3	2 + 0	4 + 4	6 + 8
6.	4 + 6	11 + 3	9 + 7	3 + 8	7 + 7	11 + 8	8 + 3	12 + 4
7.	0 + 5	10 + 1	6 + 3	2 + 6	10 + 0	7 + 6	6 + 8	7 + 4
8.	6 + 9	3 + 5	5 + 1	12 + 6	6 + 0	4 + 8	12 + 4	1 + 9
9.	1 + 5	11 + 9	9 + 1	11 + 4	5 + 7	2 + 5	7 + 9	8 + 6
10.	11 + 0	6 + 9	12 + 5	4 + 2	2 + 6	8 + 2	12 + 9	10 + 9

Math Connection—Grade 4—RBP0164   www.summerbridgeactivities.com   © RBP Books

Facts Review: Subtraction

Subtract.

1.	10 − 0	7 − 1	5 − 1	15 − 9	11 − 1	4 − 1	13 − 8	3 − 2
2.	5 − 5	14 − 5	12 − 2	6 − 1	17 − 6	9 − 1	16 − 6	8 − 5
3.	13 − 9	8 − 1	1 − 1	15 − 8	12 − 5	3 − 1	13 − 7	5 − 4
4.	17 − 7	15 − 5	13 − 4	10 − 1	5 − 2	14 − 6	4 − 2	9 − 6
5.	11 − 2	8 − 4	14 − 7	4 − 4	7 − 2	11 − 10	16 − 7	6 − 2
6.	8 − 7	16 − 8	9 − 2	17 − 8	18 − 10	10 − 8	2 − 2	12 − 4
7.	10 − 2	18 − 9	12 − 3	5 − 3	8 − 2	17 − 9	11 − 3	15 − 6
8.	14 − 9	13 − 6	6 − 3	7 − 3	14 − 8	13 − 5	16 − 9	15 − 10
9.	6 − 4	8 − 3	17 − 10	9 − 5	18 − 11	8 − 6	10 − 3	2 − 1
10.	15 − 7	9 − 7	16 − 10	11 − 4	4 − 3	13 − 10	7 − 4	14 − 10

Facts Review: Subtraction

Subtract.

1.	7 − 5	8 − 4	3 − 3	4 − 1	12 − 6	15 − 9	9 − 3	17 − 6
2.	4 − 4	14 − 10	5 − 4	10 − 9	3 − 2	11 − 5	8 − 2	12 − 11
3.	12 − 10	1 − 1	14 − 5	13 − 4	6 − 5	13 − 8	5 − 5	16 − 9
4.	8 − 3	9 − 4	15 − 5	7 − 6	16 − 6	14 − 6	10 − 7	8 − 5
5.	16 − 8	11 − 6	17 − 10	12 − 7	4 − 2	13 − 5	18 − 9	14 − 11
6.	8 − 6	2 − 1	10 − 4	14 − 7	13 − 9	7 − 7	9 − 8	5 − 2
7.	16 − 11	13 − 10	8 − 1	18 − 10	17 − 7	16 − 7	15 − 6	11 − 7
8.	14 − 9	11 − 8	15 − 7	13 − 6	10 − 5	5 − 3	4 − 3	12 − 8
9.	5 − 1	12 − 9	17 − 9	6 − 6	3 − 1	8 − 7	14 − 8	16 − 10
10.	10 − 10	13 − 7	18 − 11	10 − 6	15 − 8	11 − 9	17 − 8	9 − 9

www.summerbridgeactivities.com

Facts Review: Multiplication

Multiply.

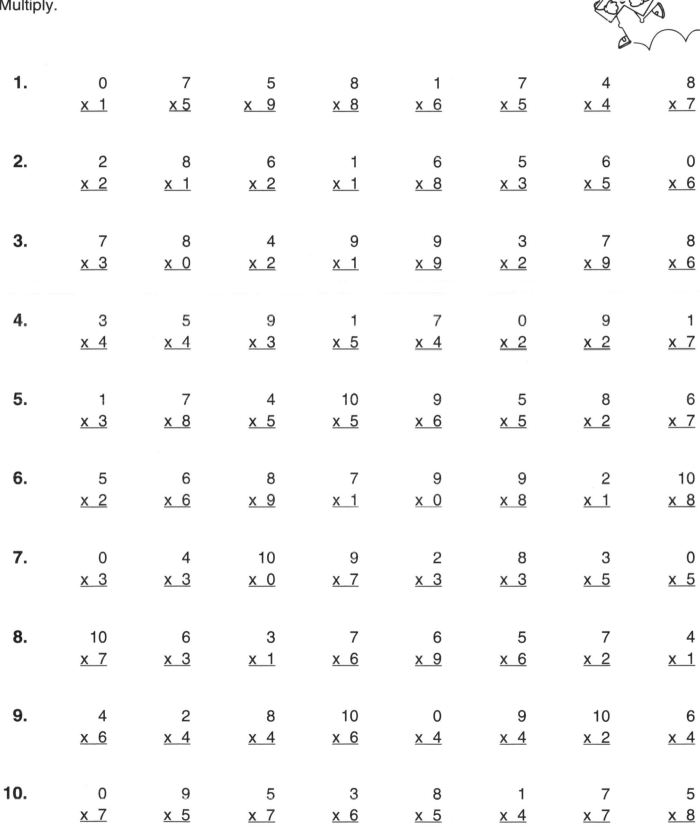

1.	0 x 1	7 x 5	5 x 9	8 x 8	1 x 6	7 x 5	4 x 4	8 x 7
2.	2 x 2	8 x 1	6 x 2	1 x 1	6 x 8	5 x 3	6 x 5	0 x 6
3.	7 x 3	8 x 0	4 x 2	9 x 1	9 x 9	3 x 2	7 x 9	8 x 6
4.	3 x 4	5 x 4	9 x 3	1 x 5	7 x 4	0 x 2	9 x 2	1 x 7
5.	1 x 3	7 x 8	4 x 5	10 x 5	9 x 6	5 x 5	8 x 2	6 x 7
6.	5 x 2	6 x 6	8 x 9	7 x 1	9 x 0	9 x 8	2 x 1	10 x 8
7.	0 x 3	4 x 3	10 x 0	9 x 7	2 x 3	8 x 3	3 x 5	0 x 5
8.	10 x 7	6 x 3	3 x 1	7 x 6	6 x 9	5 x 6	7 x 2	4 x 1
9.	4 x 6	2 x 4	8 x 4	10 x 6	0 x 4	9 x 4	10 x 2	6 x 4
10.	0 x 7	9 x 5	5 x 7	3 x 6	8 x 5	1 x 4	7 x 7	5 x 8

www.summerbridgeactivities.com

Math Connection—Grade 4—RBP0164

Facts Review: Multiplication

Multiply.

1.	5 x 2	1 x 7	9 x 1	2 x 5	10 x 9	3 x 7	7 x 7	4 x 7
2.	4 x 2	8 x 6	6 x 2	7 x 8	9 x 7	6 x 8	5 x 5	9 x 2
3.	11 x 5	6 x 7	8 x 1	4 x 8	0 x 5	1 x 8	4 x 4	8 x 5
4.	2 x 8	7 x 2	3 x 8	5 x 1	6 x 9	9 x 8	8 x 2	1 x 9
5.	8 x 9	1 x 3	5 x 6	8 x 7	2 x 6	4 x 9	7 x 6	4 x 1
6.	7 x 9	4 x 10	9 x 9	8 x 3	7 x 3	11 x 4	6 x 3	10 x 7
7.	5 x 8	9 x 4	10 x 8	2 x 7	0 x 1	3 x 9	5 x 3	0 x 5
8.	6 x 6	4 x 3	8 x 4	6 x 4	10 x 9	5 x 9	8 x 8	9 x 3
9.	10 x 3	7 x 4	5 x 4	10 x 1	9 x 5	10 x 6	5 x 7	2 x 9
10.	0 x 7	9 x 6	11 x 3	7 x 5	0 x 2	1 x 4	11 x 6	6 x 5

Math Connection—Grade 4—RBP0164   www.summerbridgeactivities.com   © RBP Books

Facts Review: Division

Divide.

1. $4\overline{)28}$ $\qquad$ $3\overline{)27}$ $\qquad$ $6\overline{)12}$ $\qquad$ $9\overline{)54}$ $\qquad$ $2\overline{)12}$

2. $7\overline{)21}$ $\qquad$ $2\overline{)10}$ $\qquad$ $5\overline{)5}$ $\qquad$ $3\overline{)24}$ $\qquad$ $8\overline{)8}$

3. $3\overline{)12}$ $\qquad$ $6\overline{)30}$ $\qquad$ $6\overline{)18}$ $\qquad$ $1\overline{)1}$ $\qquad$ $7\overline{)63}$

4. $4\overline{)20}$ $\qquad$ $9\overline{)63}$ $\qquad$ $3\overline{)6}$ $\qquad$ $9\overline{)45}$ $\qquad$ $3\overline{)15}$

5. $1\overline{)8}$ $\qquad$ $5\overline{)15}$ $\qquad$ $4\overline{)4}$ $\qquad$ $8\overline{)16}$ $\qquad$ $2\overline{)4}$

6. $3\overline{)18}$ $\qquad$ $6\overline{)54}$ $\qquad$ $1\overline{)0}$ $\qquad$ $5\overline{)30}$ $\qquad$ $9\overline{)36}$

7. $5\overline{)45}$ $\qquad$ $2\overline{)8}$ $\qquad$ $6\overline{)6}$ $\qquad$ $7\overline{)70}$ $\qquad$ $4\overline{)32}$

8. $1\overline{)12}$ $\qquad$ $8\overline{)48}$ $\qquad$ $4\overline{)16}$ $\qquad$ $7\overline{)49}$ $\qquad$ $2\overline{)14}$

9. $7\overline{)35}$ $\qquad$ $2\overline{)18}$ $\qquad$ $5\overline{)25}$ $\qquad$ $6\overline{)48}$ $\qquad$ $9\overline{)81}$

10. $1\overline{)6}$ $\qquad$ $5\overline{)55}$ $\qquad$ $8\overline{)32}$ $\qquad$ $4\overline{)36}$ $\qquad$ $2\overline{)16}$

Facts Review: Division

Divide.

1. $3\overline{)3}$ $5\overline{)10}$ $7\overline{)14}$ $1\overline{)9}$ $6\overline{)6}$

2. $5\overline{)40}$ $4\overline{)4}$ $2\overline{)2}$ $9\overline{)90}$ $8\overline{)72}$

3. $2\overline{)18}$ $9\overline{)72}$ $4\overline{)28}$ $7\overline{)63}$ $1\overline{)3}$

4. $6\overline{)12}$ $3\overline{)27}$ $7\overline{)7}$ $3\overline{)9}$ $7\overline{)49}$

5. $5\overline{)15}$ $2\overline{)6}$ $4\overline{)12}$ $9\overline{)27}$ $5\overline{)45}$

6. $3\overline{)24}$ $7\overline{)42}$ $1\overline{)4}$ $9\overline{)63}$ $2\overline{)14}$

7. $4\overline{)36}$ $8\overline{)32}$ $3\overline{)12}$ $7\overline{)21}$ $2\overline{)20}$

8. $6\overline{)42}$ $2\overline{)10}$ $6\overline{)24}$ $5\overline{)25}$ $8\overline{)40}$

9. $9\overline{)45}$ $3\overline{)21}$ $5\overline{)55}$ $4\overline{)20}$ $2\overline{)8}$

10. $5\overline{)30}$ $7\overline{)35}$ $1\overline{)10}$ $6\overline{)48}$ $3\overline{)30}$

Addition and Subtraction Chart

To add:
6 + 3 =
Find row 6 and column 3. The sum is where they intersect.
6 + 3 = **9**

To subtract:
13 − 7 =
Find 13 in column 7. Follow the row to the left edge to find the answer.
13 − 7 = **6**

+ / −	0	1	2	3	4	5	6	7	8	9	10	11	12
0	0	1	2	3	4	5	6	7	8	9	10	11	12
1	1	2	3	4	5	6	7	8	9	10	11	12	13
2	2	3	4	5	6	7	8	9	10	11	12	13	14
3	3	4	5	6	7	8	9	10	11	12	13	14	15
4	4	5	6	7	8	9	10	11	12	13	14	15	16
5	5	6	7	8	9	10	11	12	13	14	15	16	17
6	6	7	8	9	10	11	12	13	14	15	16	17	18
7	7	8	9	10	11	12	13	14	15	16	17	18	19
8	8	9	10	11	12	13	14	15	16	17	18	19	20
9	9	10	11	12	13	14	15	16	17	18	19	20	21
10	10	11	12	13	14	15	16	17	18	19	20	21	22
11	11	12	13	14	15	16	17	18	19	20	21	22	23
12	12	13	14	15	16	17	18	19	20	21	22	23	24

We love this math stuff!

www.summerbridgeactivities.com   Math Connection—Grade 4—RBP0164

Multiplication and Division Chart

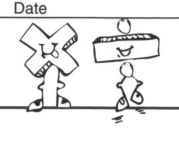

To multiply:
5 x 6 =
Find row 5 and column 6. The answer is where they intersect.
5 x 6 = **30**

To divide:
48 ÷ 6 =
Find 48 in column 6. Follow the row to the left edge to find the answer.
48 ÷ 6 = **8**

x / ÷	0	1	2	3	4	5	6	7	8	9	10	11	12
0	0	0	0	0	0	0	0	0	0	0	0	0	0
1	0	1	2	3	4	5	6	7	8	9	10	11	12
2	0	2	4	6	8	10	12	14	16	18	20	22	24
3	0	3	6	9	12	15	18	21	24	27	30	33	36
4	0	4	8	12	16	20	24	28	32	36	40	44	48
5	0	5	10	15	20	25	30	35	40	45	50	55	60
6	0	6	12	18	24	30	36	42	48	54	60	66	72
7	0	7	14	21	28	35	42	49	56	63	70	77	84
8	0	8	16	24	32	40	48	56	64	72	80	88	96
9	0	9	18	27	36	45	54	63	72	81	90	99	108
10	0	10	20	30	40	50	60	70	80	90	100	110	120
11	0	11	22	33	44	55	66	77	88	99	110	121	132
12	0	12	24	36	48	60	72	84	96	108	120	132	144

Math Connection—Grade 4—RBP0164   www.summerbridgeactivities.com   ©RBP Books

Tips for Learning Multiplication Facts

Learning multiplication facts takes practice. There are many different ways to learn and remember them. Here are just a few tricks:

- Double the 2's tables to get the 4's tables.

- Double the 4's tables to get the 8's tables.

- Memorize a table by "skip counting." For example, if you can count by 2's, you know the 2's tables.

- Look for patterns. Remember, you can switch the two factors around, and you have another multiplication fact with the same answer.

- Try making a set of flashcards. On the front of your card, write one multiplication fact. On the back, write the answer. Go through them with your friends and practice!

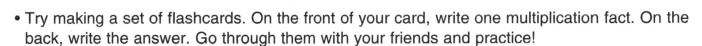

- For the 10's tables, take the number you are multiplying by 10, and add a zero.

- For the 11's tables, simply write the number you are multiplying twice (this works up to 9).

Write a 2, and then write another 2.

- Draw a picture to help you remember.

Problem Solving Strategies

There are many strategies you can use to solve problems. Sometimes there is more than one way to solve a problem, and you need to look at several possibilities.

Here are some basic strategies and questions to ask when trying to solve problems.

Investigate:

- Read the problem.
- Have you seen a problem like this one before?
- How is this problem the same, or how is this problem different?
- What information do you know?
- What information are you trying to find?

Pick a strategy for solving the problem:

- How did you work the problem like this one in the past?
- What other ways might you work the problem?
- What are the strategies you already know for solving problems?

Solve the problem:

- Try a strategy for solving the problem!

Check your work:

- Does your answer seem reasonable?
- Put the numbers from your answer back in the problem. Do they fit?

Other tips for trying to solve problems:

- Look for a pattern.
- Draw a picture.
- Make a guess or estimate, and then check your answer.
- Organize the information the problem gives you in a chart, graph, or list.
- Use objects to act out the problem as you read it.

Pre-Test: 2–Digit Addition and Subtraction with No Regrouping

Add.

1. 53 + 3	72 + 5	22 + 7	85 + 3	41 + 6	93 + 2
2. 60 + 9	21 + 4	11 + 3	80 + 2	12 + 4	81 + 7
3. 28 + 11	42 + 35	62 + 15	73 + 26	17 + 50	55 + 43
4. 64 + 25	35 + 14	57 + 40	21 + 71	69 + 20	72 + 36

Subtract.

5. 15 – 2	23 – 1	97 – 4	69 – 5	45 – 3	38 – 7
6. 85 – 5	49 – 7	67 – 3	78 – 6	98 – 7	46 – 3
7. 60 – 50	60 – 40	80 – 30	70 – 60	90 – 50	40 – 20
8. 88 – 82	76 – 35	49 – 16	99 – 72	87 – 47	64 – 31

Practice Page: 2–Digit Addition and Subtraction with No Regrouping

First add the **ones** column.	Then add the **tens** column.	First subtract the **ones** column.	Then subtract the **tens** column.
$\begin{array}{r} 2\,5 \\ +\ \ 3 \\ \hline 8 \end{array}$	$\begin{array}{r} 2\,5 \\ +\ \ 3 \\ \hline 2\,8 \end{array}$	$\begin{array}{r} 4\,9 \\ -\ \ 5 \\ \hline 4 \end{array}$	$\begin{array}{r} 4\,9 \\ -\ \ 5 \\ \hline 4\,4 \end{array}$

Add.

1.
$\begin{array}{r} 92 \\ +\ 3 \\ \hline \end{array}$
$\begin{array}{r} 57 \\ +\ 2 \\ \hline \end{array}$
$\begin{array}{r} 24 \\ +\ 5 \\ \hline \end{array}$
$\begin{array}{r} 66 \\ +\ 3 \\ \hline \end{array}$
$\begin{array}{r} 50 \\ +\ 6 \\ \hline \end{array}$
$\begin{array}{r} 11 \\ +\ 7 \\ \hline \end{array}$

2.
$\begin{array}{r} 2 \\ +\ 15 \\ \hline \end{array}$
$\begin{array}{r} 7 \\ +\ 22 \\ \hline \end{array}$
$\begin{array}{r} 3 \\ +\ 84 \\ \hline \end{array}$
$\begin{array}{r} 8 \\ +\ 31 \\ \hline \end{array}$
$\begin{array}{r} 6 \\ +\ 42 \\ \hline \end{array}$
$\begin{array}{r} 5 \\ +\ 93 \\ \hline \end{array}$

3.
$\begin{array}{r} 45 \\ +\ 2 \\ \hline \end{array}$
$\begin{array}{r} 64 \\ +\ 1 \\ \hline \end{array}$
$\begin{array}{r} 11 \\ +\ 7 \\ \hline \end{array}$
$\begin{array}{r} 90 \\ +\ 4 \\ \hline \end{array}$
$\begin{array}{r} 16 \\ +\ 3 \\ \hline \end{array}$
$\begin{array}{r} 33 \\ +\ 1 \\ \hline \end{array}$

Subtract.

4.
$\begin{array}{r} 17 \\ -\ 4 \\ \hline \end{array}$
$\begin{array}{r} 43 \\ -\ 2 \\ \hline \end{array}$
$\begin{array}{r} 64 \\ -\ 1 \\ \hline \end{array}$
$\begin{array}{r} 89 \\ -\ 4 \\ \hline \end{array}$
$\begin{array}{r} 67 \\ -\ 6 \\ \hline \end{array}$
$\begin{array}{r} 29 \\ -\ 3 \\ \hline \end{array}$

5.
$\begin{array}{r} 35 \\ -\ 4 \\ \hline \end{array}$
$\begin{array}{r} 58 \\ -\ 6 \\ \hline \end{array}$
$\begin{array}{r} 74 \\ -\ 2 \\ \hline \end{array}$
$\begin{array}{r} 36 \\ -\ 4 \\ \hline \end{array}$
$\begin{array}{r} 29 \\ -\ 8 \\ \hline \end{array}$
$\begin{array}{r} 17 \\ -\ 5 \\ \hline \end{array}$

6.
$\begin{array}{r} 11 \\ -\ 1 \\ \hline \end{array}$
$\begin{array}{r} 95 \\ -\ 2 \\ \hline \end{array}$
$\begin{array}{r} 55 \\ -\ 4 \\ \hline \end{array}$
$\begin{array}{r} 48 \\ -\ 6 \\ \hline \end{array}$
$\begin{array}{r} 67 \\ -\ 4 \\ \hline \end{array}$
$\begin{array}{r} 37 \\ -\ 5 \\ \hline \end{array}$

Math Connection—Grade 4—RBP0164   www.summerbridgeactivities.com   ©RBP Books

Practice Page: 2–Digit Addition with No Regrouping

Add.

	First add the **ones** column.	Then add the **tens** column.
	3|4 +1|2 |6	|3|4 +|1|2 |4|6

1.
72	84	34	92	65	37
+ 3	+ 3	+ 2	+ 7	+ 4	+ 2

2.
6	4	5	3	8	2
+ 23	+ 94	+ 74	+ 55	+ 30	+ 16

3.
20	40	80	70	30	60
+ 10	+ 50	+ 10	+ 20	+ 50	+ 40

4.
50	30	60	40	60	70
+ 20	+ 50	+ 20	+ 50	+ 10	+ 10

5.
11	26	36	53	24	19
+ 23	+ 13	+ 53	+ 14	+ 22	+ 60

6.
55	16	24	43	72	68
+ 12	+ 83	+ 54	+ 54	+ 26	+ 21

7.
19	46	72	65	37	57
+ 40	+ 12	+ 17	+ 33	+ 12	+ 42

www.summerbridgeactivities.com

Math Connection—Grade 4—RBP0164

Practice Page: 2–Digit Subtraction with No Regrouping

Subtract.

First subtract the **ones** column.	Then subtract the **tens** column.
$\begin{array}{r}9\,\boxed{7}\\-1\,\boxed{6}\\\hline \boxed{1}\end{array}$	$\begin{array}{r}\boxed{9}\,7\\-\ 1\,6\\\hline \boxed{8}\,1\end{array}$

1.

$\begin{array}{r}7\\-\ 3\\\hline\end{array}$	$\begin{array}{r}4\\-\ 3\\\hline\end{array}$	$\begin{array}{r}8\\-\ 6\\\hline\end{array}$	$\begin{array}{r}9\\-\ 5\\\hline\end{array}$	$\begin{array}{r}5\\-\ 2\\\hline\end{array}$	$\begin{array}{r}6\\-\ 4\\\hline\end{array}$

2.

$\begin{array}{r}29\\-\ 2\\\hline\end{array}$	$\begin{array}{r}47\\-\ 5\\\hline\end{array}$	$\begin{array}{r}35\\-\ 1\\\hline\end{array}$	$\begin{array}{r}18\\-\ 6\\\hline\end{array}$	$\begin{array}{r}24\\-\ 3\\\hline\end{array}$	$\begin{array}{r}19\\-\ 7\\\hline\end{array}$

3.

$\begin{array}{r}38\\-\ 4\\\hline\end{array}$	$\begin{array}{r}45\\-\ 3\\\hline\end{array}$	$\begin{array}{r}37\\-\ 7\\\hline\end{array}$	$\begin{array}{r}55\\-\ 3\\\hline\end{array}$	$\begin{array}{r}69\\-\ 7\\\hline\end{array}$	$\begin{array}{r}88\\-\ 2\\\hline\end{array}$

4.

$\begin{array}{r}40\\-\ 10\\\hline\end{array}$	$\begin{array}{r}70\\-\ 50\\\hline\end{array}$	$\begin{array}{r}90\\-\ 40\\\hline\end{array}$	$\begin{array}{r}80\\-\ 60\\\hline\end{array}$	$\begin{array}{r}20\\-\ 10\\\hline\end{array}$	$\begin{array}{r}50\\-\ 40\\\hline\end{array}$

5.

$\begin{array}{r}50\\-\ 10\\\hline\end{array}$	$\begin{array}{r}40\\-\ 20\\\hline\end{array}$	$\begin{array}{r}60\\-\ 40\\\hline\end{array}$	$\begin{array}{r}30\\-\ 10\\\hline\end{array}$	$\begin{array}{r}40\\-\ 30\\\hline\end{array}$	$\begin{array}{r}90\\-\ 70\\\hline\end{array}$

6.

$\begin{array}{r}78\\-\ 62\\\hline\end{array}$	$\begin{array}{r}59\\-\ 56\\\hline\end{array}$	$\begin{array}{r}67\\-\ 26\\\hline\end{array}$	$\begin{array}{r}38\\-\ 12\\\hline\end{array}$	$\begin{array}{r}19\\-\ 16\\\hline\end{array}$	$\begin{array}{r}27\\-\ 16\\\hline\end{array}$

7.

$\begin{array}{r}98\\-\ 43\\\hline\end{array}$	$\begin{array}{r}26\\-\ 14\\\hline\end{array}$	$\begin{array}{r}67\\-\ 42\\\hline\end{array}$	$\begin{array}{r}58\\-\ 25\\\hline\end{array}$	$\begin{array}{r}34\\-\ 12\\\hline\end{array}$	$\begin{array}{r}46\\-\ 23\\\hline\end{array}$

Practice Page: 2–Digit Addition and Subtraction with No Regrouping

Add.

| 1. | 14
+ 4 | 37
+ 1 | 24
+ 5 | 53
+ 3 | 42
+ 5 | 12
+ 6 |

| 2. | 3
+ 22 | 4
+ 43 | 6
+ 31 | 3
+ 53 | 7
+ 12 | 2
+ 96 |

| 3. | 21
+ 11 | 37
+ 52 | 49
+ 40 | 53
+ 24 | 25
+ 61 | 28
+ 31 |

| 4. | 19
+ 70 | 26
+ 31 | 54
+ 23 | 46
+ 21 | 35
+ 54 | 83
+ 11 |

Subtract.

| 5. | 29
– 6 | 18
– 2 | 37
– 4 | 57
– 4 | 19
– 7 | 49
– 4 |

| 6. | 50
– 30 | 40
– 10 | 60
– 40 | 30
– 10 | 60
– 20 | 70
– 50 |

| 7. | 65
– 32 | 44
– 23 | 28
– 17 | 56
– 54 | 18
– 15 | 37
– 14 |

| 8. | 56
– 13 | 68
– 27 | 44
– 42 | 79
– 64 | 38
– 22 | 97
– 25 |

www.summerbridgeactivities.com   Math Connection—Grade 4—RBP0164

Practice Page: 2–Digit Addition and Subtraction with No Regrouping

Add.

1.	$\begin{array}{r} 1 \\ + 16 \end{array}$	$\begin{array}{r} 3 \\ + 24 \end{array}$	$\begin{array}{r} 4 \\ + 34 \end{array}$	$\begin{array}{r} 2 \\ + 47 \end{array}$	$\begin{array}{r} 5 \\ + 52 \end{array}$	$\begin{array}{r} 3 \\ + 64 \end{array}$
2.	$\begin{array}{r} 25 \\ + 3 \end{array}$	$\begin{array}{r} 47 \\ + 2 \end{array}$	$\begin{array}{r} 33 \\ + 6 \end{array}$	$\begin{array}{r} 57 \\ + 1 \end{array}$	$\begin{array}{r} 63 \\ + 4 \end{array}$	$\begin{array}{r} 74 \\ + 5 \end{array}$
3.	$\begin{array}{r} 30 \\ + 20 \end{array}$	$\begin{array}{r} 40 \\ + 50 \end{array}$	$\begin{array}{r} 60 \\ + 20 \end{array}$	$\begin{array}{r} 80 \\ + 10 \end{array}$	$\begin{array}{r} 70 \\ + 20 \end{array}$	$\begin{array}{r} 50 \\ + 30 \end{array}$
4.	$\begin{array}{r} 28 \\ + 40 \end{array}$	$\begin{array}{r} 48 \\ + 21 \end{array}$	$\begin{array}{r} 65 \\ + 11 \end{array}$	$\begin{array}{r} 19 \\ + 70 \end{array}$	$\begin{array}{r} 46 \\ + 23 \end{array}$	$\begin{array}{r} 57 \\ + 41 \end{array}$

Subtract.

5.	$\begin{array}{r} 32 \\ - 1 \end{array}$	$\begin{array}{r} 49 \\ - 2 \end{array}$	$\begin{array}{r} 26 \\ - 6 \end{array}$	$\begin{array}{r} 74 \\ - 2 \end{array}$	$\begin{array}{r} 38 \\ - 6 \end{array}$	$\begin{array}{r} 29 \\ - 2 \end{array}$
6.	$\begin{array}{r} 90 \\ - 40 \end{array}$	$\begin{array}{r} 70 \\ - 20 \end{array}$	$\begin{array}{r} 60 \\ - 40 \end{array}$	$\begin{array}{r} 80 \\ - 30 \end{array}$	$\begin{array}{r} 40 \\ - 20 \end{array}$	$\begin{array}{r} 90 \\ - 50 \end{array}$
7.	$\begin{array}{r} 44 \\ - 13 \end{array}$	$\begin{array}{r} 29 \\ - 16 \end{array}$	$\begin{array}{r} 35 \\ - 11 \end{array}$	$\begin{array}{r} 19 \\ - 17 \end{array}$	$\begin{array}{r} 76 \\ - 24 \end{array}$	$\begin{array}{r} 58 \\ - 36 \end{array}$
8.	$\begin{array}{r} 84 \\ - 60 \end{array}$	$\begin{array}{r} 56 \\ - 23 \end{array}$	$\begin{array}{r} 68 \\ - 21 \end{array}$	$\begin{array}{r} 77 \\ - 50 \end{array}$	$\begin{array}{r} 57 \\ - 14 \end{array}$	$\begin{array}{r} 99 \\ - 42 \end{array}$

Math Connection—Grade 4—RBP0164   www.summerbridgeactivities.com   © RBP Books

Problem Solving: 2–Digit Addition and Subtraction with No Regrouping

Solve each problem.

1.

Rex has 17 hamsters. Lucy has 11 hamsters. How many hamsters do Rex and Lucy have altogether?

$$\begin{array}{r} 17 \\ +11 \\ \hline \textbf{28 hamsters} \end{array}$$

Remember to write the unit in your answer!

2.

The pet store has 26 rabbits and 12 guinea pigs. How many more rabbits than guinea pigs does the pet store have?

3.

Marcy has 16 goldfish in her aquarium. Jason has 29 in his aquarium. How many more goldfish does Jason have than Marcy?

4.

Jack bought 13 pounds of dog food. A week later, he bought 25 pounds of dog food. How many pounds of dog food did Jack buy altogether?

5.

Isabel's aquarium had 43 fish. She took out 12 fish. How many fish does Isabel have left in her aquarium?

6.

Dennis has 86 ants in his ant farm. Jack has 35 ants in his farm. How many more ants does Dennis have than Jack?

7.

Sarah has 58 insects in her collection. Matt has 14 fewer than Sarah. How many insects does Matt have?

8.

The pet store has 14 lizards and 5 iguanas. How many reptiles does the pet store have altogether?

© RBP Books   www.summerbridgeactivities.com   Math Connection—Grade 4—RBP0164

Problem Solving: 2–Digit Addition and Subtraction with No Regrouping

Solve each problem.

1.

Charley scored 22 more points than Luis. Luis scored 34 points. How many points did Charley score?

2.

The Panthers scored 15 more points than the Bulldogs. If the Bulldogs scored 24 points, how many points did the Panthers score?

3.

Leslie's team scored 31 fewer points at Monday's game than at Wednesday's game. If her team scored 58 points at Wednesday's game, how many points did her team score at Monday's game?

4.

Eric counted 12 points for the girls and 16 points for the boys. How many points did Eric count altogether?

5.

Jill scored 24 points on the first video game she played. She scored 14 points on the second video game. What is the total number of points Jill scored?

6.

Will scored 43 points on his first test. On his second test, he scored 53 points. How many points did Will score altogether?

7.

The Bears made 21 more baskets than the Tigers. The Tigers made 55 baskets. How many baskets did the Bears make?

8.

Shawn scored 12 points. Liz scored 15 points. How many points did Shawn and Liz score altogether?

Math Connection—Grade 4—RBP0164   www.summerbridgeactivities.com   © RBP Books

Name _____   Date _____

Post-Test: 2–Digit Addition and Subtraction with No Regrouping

Add.

1.	15 + 3	28 + 1	35 + 2	64 + 3	94 + 3	45 + 3
2.	40 + 8	11 + 5	66 + 3	53 + 4	12 + 5	72 + 3
3.	14 + 23	42 + 26	50 + 39	28 + 41	89 + 10	72 + 56
4.	35 + 42	20 + 69	67 + 11	43 + 33	84 + 15	76 + 13

Subtract.

5.	25 – 4	19 – 7	36 – 3	58 – 4	67 – 3	59 – 7
6.	43 – 2	77 – 5	19 – 6	28 – 4	55 – 3	98 – 2
7.	58 – 56	28 – 14	67 – 54	57 – 24	24 – 12	41 – 20
8.	68 – 32	85 – 34	76 – 16	89 – 26	54 – 12	82 – 41

www.summerbridgeactivities.com   Math Connection—Grade 4—RBP0164

Geometry: Identifying Shapes and Attributes of Shapes

Fill in the missing numbers that describe the polygons below.

Remember, a **polygon** has as many angles as it has sides.

Polygon	Sides	Angles	Number of Vertices
triangle	3	3	3
quadrilateral			
	5		
hexagon		6	
heptagon			
	8		

Draw a line to match each shape with its correct name.

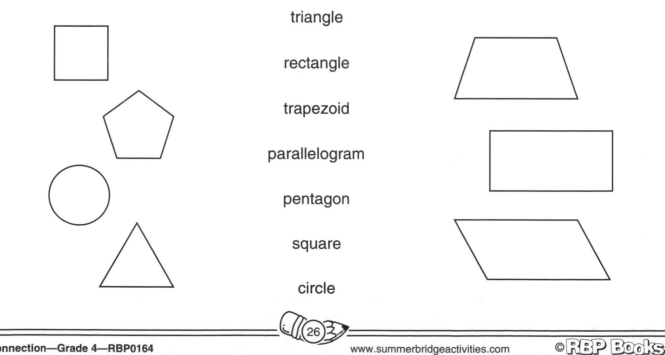

triangle

rectangle

trapezoid

parallelogram

pentagon

square

circle

Math Connection—Grade 4—RBP0164   www.summerbridgeactivities.com   © RBP Books

Name _____   Date _____

Pre-Test: 2– and 3–Digit Addition and Subtraction with Regrouping

Add.

1.
5	2	7	2	3	4
1	1	3	5	2	7
+ 4	+ 6	+ 1	+ 6	+ 2	+ 3

2.
45	15	66	58	35	79
+ 8	+ 5	+ 7	+ 4	+ 6	+ 3

3.
16	28	76	18	47	39
+ 39	+ 56	+ 48	+ 94	+ 57	+ 88

4.
28	84	67	15	34	73
35	20	59	49	65	14
+ 70	+ 16	+ 22	+ 32	+ 18	+ 25

Subtract.

5.
15	24	41	83	54	62
– 6	– 5	– 9	– 4	– 9	– 7

6.
21	62	74	47	82	54
– 12	– 48	– 39	– 19	– 58	– 27

7.
183	342	531	818	652	726
– 48	– 36	– 15	– 34	– 27	– 42

8.
840	517	411	607	813	364
– 24	– 83	– 29	– 249	– 457	– 275

www.summerbridgeactivities.com   **Math Connection—Grade 4—RBP0164**

Practice Page: 2– and 3–Digit Addition with Regrouping

Add.

First add the **ones** column, and regroup.

$$\begin{array}{r} {}^{1}3\,|\,5 \\ +\ 2\,|\,7 \\ \hline 2 \end{array}$$

Then add the **tens** column.

$$\begin{array}{r} {}^{1}3\,|\,5 \\ +\ 2\,|\,7 \\ \hline 6\,|\,2 \end{array}$$

1.

24	19	37	19	27	38
+ 7	+ 5	+ 3	+ 6	+ 4	+ 3

2.

8	9	2	6	5	9
+ 46	+ 23	+ 89	+ 37	+ 18	+ 26

3.

27	43	57	18	64	25
+ 47	+ 29	+ 34	+ 25	+ 17	+ 55

4.

16	37	64	17	54	45
+ 18	+ 46	+ 19	+ 39	+ 26	+ 29

5.

36	24	37	66	53	74
+ 57	+ 68	+ 43	+ 29	+ 39	+ 19

6.

19	26	18	36	28	46
+ 35	+ 47	+ 77	+ 19	+ 16	+ 39

7.

58	29	46	55	86	79
+ 26	+ 45	+ 39	+ 29	+ 16	+ 19

Practice Page: 2–Digit Addition with Regrouping

Add.

First add the **ones** column, and regroup.	Then add the **tens** column.
$\begin{array}{r}{}^1 1\,2\\2\,4\\+\,1\,5\\\hline 1\end{array}$	$\begin{array}{r}{}^1 1\,2\\2\,4\\+\,1\,5\\\hline 5\,1\end{array}$

1.
$$\begin{array}{r}6\\4\\+\,4\\\hline\end{array}\qquad \begin{array}{r}9\\5\\+\,3\\\hline\end{array}\qquad \begin{array}{r}2\\8\\+\,1\\\hline\end{array}\qquad \begin{array}{r}7\\6\\+\,3\\\hline\end{array}\qquad \begin{array}{r}4\\5\\+\,7\\\hline\end{array}\qquad \begin{array}{r}9\\8\\+\,4\\\hline\end{array}$$

2.
$$\begin{array}{r}8\\6\\+\,6\\\hline\end{array}\qquad \begin{array}{r}3\\9\\+\,9\\\hline\end{array}\qquad \begin{array}{r}4\\5\\+\,9\\\hline\end{array}\qquad \begin{array}{r}8\\9\\+\,8\\\hline\end{array}\qquad \begin{array}{r}6\\5\\+\,9\\\hline\end{array}\qquad \begin{array}{r}7\\3\\+\,8\\\hline\end{array}$$

3.
$$\begin{array}{r}43\\11\\+\,27\\\hline\end{array}\qquad \begin{array}{r}24\\18\\+\,37\\\hline\end{array}\qquad \begin{array}{r}25\\17\\+\,32\\\hline\end{array}\qquad \begin{array}{r}18\\39\\+\,26\\\hline\end{array}\qquad \begin{array}{r}38\\19\\+\,26\\\hline\end{array}\qquad \begin{array}{r}17\\18\\+\,16\\\hline\end{array}$$

4.
$$\begin{array}{r}34\\26\\+\,18\\\hline\end{array}\qquad \begin{array}{r}25\\35\\+\,46\\\hline\end{array}\qquad \begin{array}{r}16\\37\\+\,42\\\hline\end{array}\qquad \begin{array}{r}28\\47\\+\,32\\\hline\end{array}\qquad \begin{array}{r}36\\17\\+\,37\\\hline\end{array}\qquad \begin{array}{r}38\\28\\+\,35\\\hline\end{array}$$

5.
$$\begin{array}{r}64\\33\\+\,71\\\hline\end{array}\qquad \begin{array}{r}12\\54\\+\,60\\\hline\end{array}\qquad \begin{array}{r}91\\97\\+\,61\\\hline\end{array}\qquad \begin{array}{r}43\\60\\+\,42\\\hline\end{array}\qquad \begin{array}{r}54\\93\\+\,31\\\hline\end{array}\qquad \begin{array}{r}92\\73\\+\,44\\\hline\end{array}$$

6.
$$\begin{array}{r}22\\63\\+\,92\\\hline\end{array}\qquad \begin{array}{r}50\\94\\+\,64\\\hline\end{array}\qquad \begin{array}{r}45\\82\\+\,52\\\hline\end{array}\qquad \begin{array}{r}86\\91\\+\,32\\\hline\end{array}\qquad \begin{array}{r}21\\35\\+\,91\\\hline\end{array}\qquad \begin{array}{r}73\\36\\+\,60\\\hline\end{array}$$

Practice Page: 2–Digit Addition with Regrouping

Add.

1.	27	48	35	93	73	62
	+ 67	+ 98	+ 76	+ 46	+ 88	+ 49

2.	62	96	18	47	86	38
	+ 58	+ 76	+ 96	+ 59	+ 49	+ 67

3.	56	49	35	68	88	95
	+ 97	+ 85	+ 78	+ 47	+ 54	+ 87

4.	85	22	19	58	49	74
	+ 27	+ 79	+ 94	+ 66	+ 93	+ 48

5.	67	52	81	44	58	96
	39	59	96	79	96	77
	+ 76	+ 84	+ 65	+ 48	+ 37	+ 49

6.	27	53	45	86	24	73
	63	94	87	99	37	38
	+ 96	+ 64	+ 53	+ 34	+ 98	+ 66

7.	29	80	18	75	92	43
	74	99	98	59	67	97
	+ 33	+ 47	+ 64	+ 43	+ 39	+ 16

Math Connection—Grade 4—RBP0164   www.summerbridgeactivities.com   © RBP Books

Practice Page: 2– and 3–Digit Subtraction with Regrouping

Subtract.

$$
\begin{array}{r} 62 \\ -\ 7 \\ \hline \end{array}
$$

Regroup 6 tens and 2 ones as 5 tens and 12 ones. Subtract the **ones** column.

$$
\begin{array}{r} {}^{5}\!\!\not{6}\,{}^{1}2 \\ -\quad\ 7 \\ \hline 5 \end{array}
$$

Subtract the **tens** column.

$$
\begin{array}{r} {}^{5}\!\!\not{6}\,{}^{1}2 \\ -\quad\ 7 \\ \hline 5\ 5 \end{array}
$$

1.

13	37	64	20	45	65
− 6	− 9	− 8	− 4	− 7	− 9

2.

52	31	60	22	15	43
− 4	− 6	− 6	− 7	− 9	− 7

3.

64	42	56	33	72	26
− 19	− 27	− 38	− 14	− 25	− 18

4.

28	32	44	94	57	82
− 19	− 29	− 37	− 38	− 29	− 46

5.

67	75	38	40	82	53
− 29	− 58	− 29	− 26	− 45	− 17

6.

280	337	262	431	845	695
− 56	− 18	− 28	− 16	− 27	− 38

www.summerbridgeactivities.com

Math Connection—Grade 4—RBP0164

Practice Page: 2– and 3–Digit Subtraction with Regrouping

Subtract.

	Regroup 4 tens and 6 ones as 3 tens and 16 ones. Subtract the **ones** column.	Regroup 4 hundreds and 3 tens as 3 hundreds and 13 tens. Subtract the **tens** column.	Subtract the **hundreds** column.
446 − 57	3 44̸6̸ − 5 7 9	3 13 4̸4̸6̸ − 5 7 8 9	3 13 4̸4̸6̸ − 5 7 3 8 9

1. 129   204   215   146   318   618
       − 62 − 43 − 91 − 77 − 36 − 51

2. 507   238   357   466   683   908
       − 82 − 43 − 69 − 82 − 92 − 17

3. 229   837   687   548   936   434
       − 46 − 45 − 94 − 93 − 64 − 92

4. 378   604   476   611   964   137
       − 99 − 17 − 77 − 42 − 37 − 79

5. 100   423   630   224   576   731
       − 48 − 78 − 15 − 92 − 89 − 20

6. 647   502   157   367   960   729
       − 87 − 35 − 92 − 48 − 56 − 56

Name _____   Date _____

Practice Page: 2– and 3–Digit Addition and Subtraction with Regrouping

Add.

1. 58 + 94	67 + 87	97 + 89	93 + 182	37 + 267	75 + 843
2. 952 + 27	629 + 79	367 + 97	814 + 86	762 + 79	569 + 97
3. 35 27 + 67	60 79 + 88	35 67 + 89	63 98 + 87	18 67 + 53	64 53 + 45
4. 45 59 + 26	87 49 + 53	26 77 + 66	94 59 + 76	24 67 + 54	99 87 + 53

Subtract.

5. 34 − 27	72 − 19	54 − 29	27 − 18	44 − 26	63 − 46
6. 641 − 29	477 − 68	276 − 57	821 − 19	650 − 36	765 − 47
7. 264 − 63	713 − 48	547 − 29	611 − 35	305 − 16	900 − 78
8. 497 − 98	132 − 67	946 − 87	761 − 83	218 − 29	608 − 99

© RBP Books   www.summerbridgeactivities.com   Math Connection—Grade 4—RBP0164

Practice Page: 2– and 3–Digit Addition and Subtraction with Regrouping

Add.

1.	8 5 + 9	6 7 + 7	2 7 + 8	2 8 + 4	3 7 + 8	4 9 + 6

2.	95 + 5	73 + 4	38 + 8	24 + 9	68 + 7	56 + 5

3.	97 + 27	28 + 46	84 + 43	17 + 95	88 + 27	58 + 73

4.	24 68 + 87	55 79 + 24	37 19 + 45	56 11 + 67	24 33 + 89	17 28 + 46

Subtract.

5.	27 − 9	64 − 7	31 − 5	55 − 6	72 − 3	90 − 6

6.	42 − 24	31 − 16	53 − 47	62 − 38	21 − 15	44 − 26

7.	60 − 17	27 − 19	42 − 34	78 − 49	34 − 18	85 − 49

8.	164 − 27	373 − 18	561 − 36	680 − 23	221 − 18	760 − 47

Math Connection—Grade 4—RBP0164   www.summerbridgeactivities.com   © RBP Books

Problem Solving: 2– and 3–Digit Addition and Subtraction with Regrouping

Solve each problem.

1.

The zoo has 113 reptiles and 74 mammals. How many more reptiles than mammals does the zoo have?

2.

Alex took 17 pictures of tigers, 32 pictures of birds, and 28 pictures of reptiles. How many pictures did Alex take altogether?

3.

Keshia talks to the zookeeper about what the zoo's penguins are fed. The penguins eat 365 pounds of fish in the spring and 437 pounds of fish in the summer. How many pounds of fish do the penguins eat altogether?

4.

Jason fed the bears 649 pounds of food in March. In April, Jason fed the bears 587 pounds of food. How many pounds of food did Jason feed the bears total?

5.

Ryan counted 18 green lizards, 27 snakes, and 36 Gila monsters. How many reptiles did he see?

6.

On Tuesday, 992 people visited the zoo. On Thursday, 749 people visited the zoo. How many more people visited the zoo on Tuesday than Thursday?

7.

Andy cleaned 59 cages on Monday, 63 cages on Tuesday, and 48 cages on Wednesday. How many cages did Andy clean altogether?

8.

Lisa walked 47 feet to see the leopards, 129 feet to see the alligators, and 86 feet to see the monkeys. How many feet did Lisa walk in all?

www.summerbridgeactivities.com **Math Connection—Grade 4—RBP0164**

Problem Solving: 2– and 3–Digit Addition and Subtraction with Regrouping

Solve each problem.

1.

Alice buys 23 gold stickers, 37 purple stickers, and 19 silver stickers. How many stickers does Alice buy altogether?

2.

Stuart buys 149 marbles. Jan buys 76 marbles. How many more marbles does Stuart buy than Jan?

3.

Max has 217 baseball cards in his collection. If Max sells 128 baseball cards, how many cards does he have left?

4.

Alex buys 349 paper clips and 34 pencils. How many office supplies does Alex buy altogether?

5.

Maria buys 49 stamps. Janice buys 27 more stamps than Maria. How many stamps does Janice buy?

6.

Gary buys 39 jelly beans and 43 gumdrops. How many pieces of candy does Gary buy altogether?

7.

Mike collects baseball cards. He spends $58.27 on a rookie card. Then, he spends $74.93 on his favorite pitcher card. How much does Mike spend on baseball cards?

8.

Amanda had $50.45 in her checking account. She deposited $27.94. Then, she bought a CD for $18.32. How much money does she have left in her checking account?

Post-Test: 2– and 3–Digit Addition and Subtraction with Regrouping

Add.

1. $\begin{array}{r} 37 \\ +\ 4 \\ \hline \end{array}$	$\begin{array}{r} 28 \\ +\ 7 \\ \hline \end{array}$	$\begin{array}{r} 56 \\ +\ 4 \\ \hline \end{array}$	$\begin{array}{r} 19 \\ +\ 9 \\ \hline \end{array}$	$\begin{array}{r} 73 \\ +\ 8 \\ \hline \end{array}$	$\begin{array}{r} 48 \\ +\ 9 \\ \hline \end{array}$
2. $\begin{array}{r} 37 \\ +\ 57 \\ \hline \end{array}$	$\begin{array}{r} 45 \\ +\ 66 \\ \hline \end{array}$	$\begin{array}{r} 58 \\ +\ 74 \\ \hline \end{array}$	$\begin{array}{r} 73 \\ +\ 98 \\ \hline \end{array}$	$\begin{array}{r} 64 \\ +\ 57 \\ \hline \end{array}$	$\begin{array}{r} 87 \\ +\ 96 \\ \hline \end{array}$
3. $\begin{array}{r} 348 \\ +\ 64 \\ \hline \end{array}$	$\begin{array}{r} 598 \\ +\ 42 \\ \hline \end{array}$	$\begin{array}{r} 198 \\ +\ 73 \\ \hline \end{array}$	$\begin{array}{r} 267 \\ +\ 65 \\ \hline \end{array}$	$\begin{array}{r} 667 \\ +\ 89 \\ \hline \end{array}$	$\begin{array}{r} 897 \\ +\ 38 \\ \hline \end{array}$
4. $\begin{array}{r} 24 \\ 45 \\ +\ 39 \\ \hline \end{array}$	$\begin{array}{r} 51 \\ 29 \\ +\ 64 \\ \hline \end{array}$	$\begin{array}{r} 88 \\ 53 \\ +\ 79 \\ \hline \end{array}$	$\begin{array}{r} 32 \\ 48 \\ +\ 94 \\ \hline \end{array}$	$\begin{array}{r} 66 \\ 80 \\ +\ 79 \\ \hline \end{array}$	$\begin{array}{r} 97 \\ 63 \\ +\ 15 \\ \hline \end{array}$

Subtract.

5. $\begin{array}{r} 55 \\ -\ 27 \\ \hline \end{array}$	$\begin{array}{r} 87 \\ -\ 48 \\ \hline \end{array}$	$\begin{array}{r} 63 \\ -\ 16 \\ \hline \end{array}$	$\begin{array}{r} 46 \\ -\ 28 \\ \hline \end{array}$	$\begin{array}{r} 92 \\ -\ 75 \\ \hline \end{array}$	$\begin{array}{r} 43 \\ -\ 29 \\ \hline \end{array}$
6. $\begin{array}{r} 550 \\ -\ 16 \\ \hline \end{array}$	$\begin{array}{r} 361 \\ -\ 29 \\ \hline \end{array}$	$\begin{array}{r} 152 \\ -\ 19 \\ \hline \end{array}$	$\begin{array}{r} 497 \\ -\ 79 \\ \hline \end{array}$	$\begin{array}{r} 264 \\ -\ 28 \\ \hline \end{array}$	$\begin{array}{r} 890 \\ -\ 57 \\ \hline \end{array}$
7. $\begin{array}{r} 641 \\ -\ 80 \\ \hline \end{array}$	$\begin{array}{r} 711 \\ -\ 84 \\ \hline \end{array}$	$\begin{array}{r} 924 \\ -\ 67 \\ \hline \end{array}$	$\begin{array}{r} 245 \\ -\ 84 \\ \hline \end{array}$	$\begin{array}{r} 508 \\ -\ 49 \\ \hline \end{array}$	$\begin{array}{r} 763 \\ -\ 18 \\ \hline \end{array}$

Probability

Alex has 7 marbles in his bag. Two marbles are red, 4 marbles are blue, and 1 marble is yellow.	The probability that Alex would pull a **red** marble out of the bag is $\frac{2}{7}$ because 2 of the 7 marbles are red.

Probability is the chance or possibility that an event will happen.

$\frac{2}{7}$ The **numerator** tells the number of possible chances that a specific thing will happen.
The **denominator** tells the total number of possible things that could happen.

- The probability that Alex would pull a **blue** marble out of the bag is $\frac{4}{7}$ because 4 of the 7 marbles are blue.

- The probability that he would pull a **yellow** marble out of the bag is $\frac{1}{7}$ because 1 of the 7 marbles is yellow.

Solve each problem.

Greta has 11 marbles in her bag. Three marbles are purple, 2 marbles are red, 1 marble is green, and 5 marbles are orange.

1. How many marbles are in Greta's bag?

2. How many orange marbles are in her bag?

3. What is the probability that Greta will pull out an orange marble?

4. What is the probability that Greta will pull out a purple marble?

5. What is the probability that Greta will pull out a green marble?

6. What is the probability that Greta will pull out a red marble?

7. What is the probability that Greta will pull out a black marble?

8. What is the probability that Greta will pull out a green or a red marble?

Pre-Test: 3– and 4–Digit Addition and Subtraction with Regrouping

Add.

1.	327 + 751	165 + 335	832 + 219	155 + 182	594 + 274	809 + 614
2.	2,716 + 8,490	6,091 + 1,363	3,917 + 6,643	1,254 + 8,458	9,525 + 7,071	4,831 + 1,716
3.	19 45 + 69	80 47 + 24	678 931 + 761	942 705 + 649	5,971 6,798 + 1,264	6,498 1,057 + 4,341
4.	15 25 13 + 40	30 34 15 + 10	231 420 300 + 113	205 413 223 + 111	2,113 2,341 1,121 + 1,030	2,214 1,340 3,101 + 2,513

Subtract.

5.	258 – 107	349 – 139	448 – 139	630 – 128	864 – 249	579 – 293
6.	1,358 – 249	3,489 – 196	5,059 – 237	2,434 – 126	3,971 – 759	8,934 – 648
7.	2,469 – 1,254	7,864 – 2,580	5,132 – 4,023	3,687 – 1,986	9,168 – 5,493	1,548 – 1,289
8.	36,479 – 2,356	14,567 – 13,459	46,987 – 4,819	24,084 – 2,892	53,173 – 5,042	94,672 – 2,891

       www.summerbridgeactivities.com   Math Connection—Grade 4—RBP0164

Practice Page: 3– and 4–Digit Addition and Subtraction with Regrouping

Add the **ones** column.	Add the **tens** column.	Add the **hundreds** column.	Subtract the **ones** column.	Regroup the **tens** column and subtract.	Subtract the **hundreds** column.
16[3] + 48[2] ____[5]	¹1[6]3 + 4[8]2 ___[4]5	¹1[6 3] + 4[8 2] [6 4 5]	51[2] − 24[1] ___[1]	⁴5¹1 2 − 2 4 1 ___7 1	⁴5¹1 2 − 2 4 1 2 7 1

Add.

1.   231   461   647   513   767   354
       + 762   + 329   + 282   + 864   + 350   + 937

2.   598   318   667   467   873   248
       + 324   + 487   + 571   + 664   + 168   + 367

3.   317   466   504   846   496   651
       + 218   + 871   + 947   + 516   + 570   + 947

Subtract.

4.   597   618   381   947   265
       − 162   − 209   − 159   − 763   − 177

5. 1,471   2,284   1,248   1,420   2,019
       − 254   − 743   − 726   − 803   − 249

6. 2,000   3,164   1,907   2,546   1,644
       − 637   − 726   − 267   − 467   − 795

7. 1,543   1,986   1,762   1,400   3,410
       − 942   − 898   − 781   − 621   − 348

Name _____ Date _____

Practice Page: 3–, 4–, and 5–Digit Addition and Subtraction with Regrouping

Add the ones column.	Add the tens column.	Add the hundreds column.	Add the thousands column.	Regroup and subtract the ones column	Subtract the tens column.	Subtract the hundreds column.	Subtract the thousands column.
4,02**7** + 8,48**2** **9**	¹ 4,0**27** + 8,4**82** **09**	¹ 4,**027** + 8,**482** **509**	¹ **4,027** + **8,482** **12,509**	5 1 9,8**6̸1** − 7,53**9** **2**	5 1 9,8**6̸1** − 7,5**39** **22**	5 1 9,8**6̸1** − 7,**539** **322**	5 1 **9,8̸6̸1** − **7,539** **2,322**

Add.

1.
1,676	3,873	6,824	4,357	2,164	5,324
+ 243	+ 129	+ 359	+ 937	+ 396	+ 907

2.
3,674	1,786	4,364	7,354	6,537	2,561
+ 1,218	+ 316	+ 7,129	+ 4,166	+ 2,845	+ 3,674

3.
5,637	8,371	2,687	4,698	5,307	7,543
+ 6,631	+ 4,929	+ 4,982	+ 1,279	+ 6,379	+ 3,178

Subtract.

4.
3,217	2,346	7,652	6,718	2,736
− 304	− 273	− 419	− 509	− 918

5.
2,647	1,966	4,645	7,668	3,744
− 1,328	− 1,248	− 3,927	− 2,880	− 1,656

6.
27,437	63,476	56,073	36,427	42,578
− 3,129	− 4,147	− 3,747	− 4,686	− 8,724

Practice Page: 3– and 4–Digit Addition with Regrouping

Add.

```
    2 2 1
  2,764   Add the ones column.
  1,942   Add the tens column.
  1,766   Add the hundreds column.
+ 5,147   Add the thousands column.
 11,619
```

1.

21	30	24	23	15
16	13	11	40	61
+ 12	+ 24	+ 36	+ 72	+ 52

2.

16	42	32	51	34
11	10	23	16	43
+ 252	+ 344	+ 137	+ 627	+ 317

3.

234	324	103	311	430
211	543	341	216	132
+ 340	+ 121	+ 234	+ 456	+ 373

4.

3,241	6,930	4,351	7,684	5,901
5,017	1,347	1,527	3,293	1,432
+ 4,538	+ 6,121	+ 7,621	+ 1,240	+ 3,542

5.

1,203	1,354	3,246	2,330	3,641
2,341	2,013	1,342	2,142	1,334
1,421	2,134	2,130	2,314	2,310
+ 3,423	+ 1,116	+ 1,011	+ 1,240	+ 4,022

6.

3,642	5,627	1,543	2,356	5,102
1,230	3,052	3,204	1,021	1,642
1,347	2,361	5,421	4,320	1,324
+ 2,357	+ 1,364	+ 2,063	+ 3,146	+ 3,516

Math Connection—Grade 4—RBP0164   www.summerbridgeactivities.com   © RBP Books

Name _____   Date _____

Practice Page: 3– and 4–Digit Addition with Regrouping
Add.

1.

12	35	34	50	13
14	30	22	42	62
+ 34	+ 6	+ 60	+ 56	+ 47

2.

354	132	253	624	450
41	30	34	13	26
+ 24	+ 77	+ 61	+ 38	+ 61

3.

214	324	624	734	344
136	241	131	230	103
+ 324	+ 345	+ 410	+ 373	+ 624

4.

3,246	6,324	2,354	3,413	2,436
4,131	1,347	1,034	6,341	4,064
+ 2,134	+ 2,341	+ 4,316	+ 7,642	+ 1,483

5.

2,341	7,341	1,209	5,442	1,023
3,456	2,683	3,416	1,330	3,542
1,348	2,134	1,221	1,342	2,134
+ 2,367	+ 2,011	+ 1,354	+ 6,341	+ 7,241

6.

3,541	1,302	1,463	3,621	4,621
1,204	4,211	4,231	1,241	3,024
2,301	5,140	3,141	2,314	3,647
+ 20,143	+ 35,333	+ 53,410	+ 44,213	+ 61,213

www.summerbridgeactivities.com   Math Connection—Grade 4—RBP0164

Practice Page: 3–, 4–, and 5–Digit Addition and Subtraction with Regrouping

Add.

1.
227	134	234	761	637
+ 347	+ 248	+ 639	+ 697	+ 841

2.
2,341	6,731	4,387	1,369	3,877
+ 671	+ 294	+ 264	+ 619	+ 862

3.
3,674	8,371	7,367	2,776	7,540
+ 6,727	+ 7,467	+ 4,672	+ 3,727	+ 5,751

4.
1,324	6,371	334	673	3,541
2,149	1,423	413	231	1,221
+ 4,371	+ 8,094	157	504	6,110
		+ 304	+ 131	+ 3,314

Subtract.

5.
347	473	632	162	564
– 225	– 392	– 260	– 139	– 187

6.
3,674	5,371	7,384	3,972	6,047
– 426	– 671	– 538	– 586	– 165

7.
6,378	7,097	3,297	6,724	4,007
– 1,048	– 2,176	– 1,368	– 3,655	– 1,374

8.
87,346	46,797	53,971	36,794	16,700
– 2,138	– 7,834	– 2,699	– 4,878	– 4,965

Math Connection—Grade 4—RBP0164   www.summerbridgeactivities.com   © RBP Books

Problem Solving: 3–, 4–, and 5–Digit Addition and Subtraction with Regrouping

Solve each problem.

1.

The ToyTime toy factory made 1,492 yellow yo-yos and 4,201 red yo-yos. How many more red yo-yos were made than yellow yo-yos?

2.

Sarah has 246 animal stickers and 432 flower stickers. How many stickers does Sarah have altogether?

3.

Tyler has 1,867 marbles. Emily has 798 marbles. How many more marbles does Tyler have than Emily?

4.

Kevin and his friends kept track of how far they flew their model airplanes. Josh flew his plane 549 feet. Annie flew hers 418 feet. Kevin flew his plane 376 feet. How many feet did their airplanes fly altogether?

5.

The ToyTime factory made 1,648 board games, 2,190 dolls, and 4,018 race cars. How many toys did they make in all?

6.

Tyler drove his toy car 1,089 inches. Alexis drove her toy car 2,802 inches. How many more inches did Alexis drive her car than Tyler?

7.

The ToyTime Web site had 631 visitors in 1 week. If the same number of people visited their website each week, how many people visited the site in 3 weeks?

8.

Jack has $20.00 in his pocket. He spends $1.16 playing video games and $2.59 on comic books. How much money does Jack have left?

www.summerbridgeactivities.com   Math Connection—Grade 4—RBP0164

Problem Solving: 3–, 4–, and 5–Digit Addition and Subtraction with Regrouping

Solve each problem.

1.
Stuart counted 5,671 red ants. Alice counted 6,105 black ants. How many more black ants than red ants were counted?

2.
The Pets-R-Us pet store sold 733 pounds of birdseed in January. In February, the store sold 559 pounds of birdseed. How many pounds of birdseed did the store sell altogether?

3.
The robin flew 3,419 feet. The blue jay flew 2,866 feet. How many more feet did the robin fly than the blue jay?

4.
At the butterfly exhibit, Ryan saw 219 orange butterflies and 859 yellow butterflies. How many butterflies did Ryan see altogether?

5.
There were 23,416 leaf cutter ants in the rain forest. There were 16,980 beetles and 5,688 dragonflies. How many insects were there altogether?

6.
9,717 birds flew south for the winter. Another 459 birds flew south. How many birds flew south altogether?

7.
There are 256 grasshoppers in the garden. If there are 2,041 insects in the garden, how many insects are not grasshoppers?

8.
Leslie saw 108 monarch butterflies in the field. Max saw 849 monarch butterflies in the meadow. How many monarch butterflies did Leslie and Max see in all?

Math Connection—Grade 4—RBP0164   www.summerbridgeactivities.com   ©RBP Books

Post-Test: 3–, 4–, and 5–Digit Addition and Subtraction with Regrouping

Add.

1.	344 + 251	467 + 139	267 + 149	3,787 + 147	6,971 + 534

2.	2,748 + 2,147	5,471 + 2,787	4,387 + 1,349	3,661 + 2,677	6,378 + 28,920

3.	36 74 + 67	13 71 + 74	73 27 + 46	272 156 + 38	5,401 6,372 + 7,514

4.	13 24 21 + 437	63 71 14 + 680	33 41 17 + 304	143 674 231 + 341	3,641 1,032 3,541 + 6,324

Subtract.

5.	653 − 241	364 − 192	467 − 284	613 − 267	504 − 283

6.	2,017 − 415	6,411 − 4,254	5,068 − 2,219	35,407 − 4,761	51,734 − 2,516

Measurement: Inches, Feet, Yards, Miles

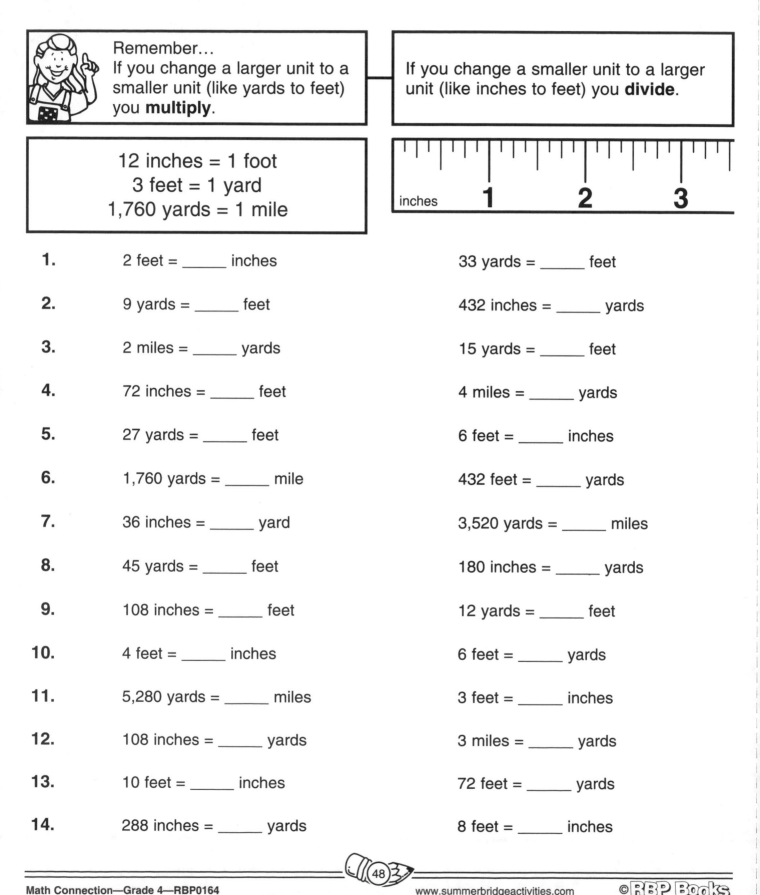

Remember…
If you change a larger unit to a smaller unit (like yards to feet) you **multiply**.

If you change a smaller unit to a larger unit (like inches to feet) you **divide**.

12 inches = 1 foot
3 feet = 1 yard
1,760 yards = 1 mile

inches **1** **2** **3**

1.   2 feet = _____ inches

2.   9 yards = _____ feet

3.   2 miles = _____ yards

4.   72 inches = _____ feet

5.   27 yards = _____ feet

6.   1,760 yards = _____ mile

7.   36 inches = _____ yard

8.   45 yards = _____ feet

9.   108 inches = _____ feet

10. 4 feet = _____ inches

11. 5,280 yards = _____ miles

12. 108 inches = _____ yards

13. 10 feet = _____ inches

14. 288 inches = _____ yards

33 yards = _____ feet

432 inches = _____ yards

15 yards = _____ feet

4 miles = _____ yards

6 feet = _____ inches

432 feet = _____ yards

3,520 yards = _____ miles

180 inches = _____ yards

12 yards = _____ feet

6 feet = _____ yards

3 feet = _____ inches

3 miles = _____ yards

72 feet = _____ yards

8 feet = _____ inches

Measurement: Inches, Feet, Yards, Miles

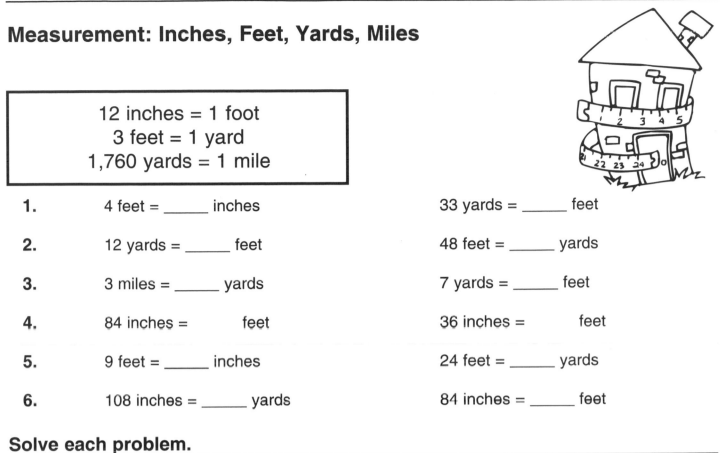

> 12 inches = 1 foot
> 3 feet = 1 yard
> 1,760 yards = 1 mile

1.   4 feet = _____ inches   33 yards = _____ feet

2.   12 yards = _____ feet   48 feet = _____ yards

3.   3 miles = _____ yards   7 yards = _____ feet

4.   84 inches =   feet   36 inches =   feet

5.   9 feet = _____ inches   24 feet = _____ yards

6.   108 inches = _____ yards   84 inches = _____ feet

Solve each problem.

7.
Leslie ran 3,520 yards. How many miles did she run?

8.
Anita has 7 yards of fabric. How many feet of fabric does she have?

9.
Brian needs 108 inches of pipe. How many feet of pipe does he need to buy?

10.
Tess has 180 inches of ribbon. She uses 36 inches. How many yards of ribbon does she have left?

11.
Mario is putting string on his kites. He needs 100 inches of string for the blue kite, 125 inches of string for the red kite, and 99 inches of string for the purple kite. How many yards of string should he buy?

12.
Gary runs 5,280 yards. How many miles does he run?

Measurement: Inches, Feet, Yards, Miles

Remember…
If you change a larger unit to a smaller unit (like yards to feet) you **multiply**.

If you change a smaller unit to a larger unit (like inches to feet) you **divide**.

12 inches = 1 foot
3 feet = 1 yard
1,760 yards = 1 mile

inches   **1**   **2**   **3**

1.
Sam drove 8,800 yards. How many miles did he drive?

2.
Lance needs 72 inches of rope. How many yards does he need to buy?

3.
Maggie is carpeting her hall. The length of the hall is 14 feet. Carpet is sold by the yard. How many yards does Maggie need to buy so she will have enough?

4.
The train track is 5,280 yards long. How many miles is the train track?

5.
Andrea buys 9 yards of fabric. How many feet of fabric does she have?

6.
Josh is 5 feet and 11 inches tall. How many inches tall is Josh?

7.
Jennifer is reading her map. Which is the shorter distance, 5 miles or 10,560 yards?

8.
Emma is sewing trim on some blankets. She needs 79 inches of trim for the first blanket, 91 inches of trim for the second, and 82 inches for the third. How many yards of trim does she need to buy?

Math Connection—Grade 4—RBP0164   www.summerbridgeactivities.com   ©RBP Books

Pre-Test: 2– and 3–Digit Multiplication by 1 Digit
Multiply.

1.	13 x 2	11 x 7	32 x 3	12 x 4	20 x 3	31 x 2
2.	24 x 2	30 x 2	11 x 4	24 x 2	42 x 3	22 x 3
3.	16 x 2	12 x 7	38 x 2	29 x 3	12 x 8	17 x 5
4.	30 x 7	11 x 6	40 x 5	11 x 3	80 x 7	45 x 2
5.	84 x 2	43 x 9	57 x 6	38 x 4	46 x 5	26 x 8
6.	130 x 2	300 x 3	101 x 4	200 x 6	504 x 2	124 x 2
7.	208 x 3	419 x 2	513 x 4	847 x 2	163 x 2	519 x 3
8.	962 x 5	155 x 2	645 x 3	872 x 3	173 x 9	931 x 7
9.	547 x 7	871 x 9	548 x 5	482 x 6	687 x 4	297 x 3

© RBP Books   www.summerbridgeactivities.com   Math Connection—Grade 4—RBP0164

Practice Page: 2–Digit Multiplication by 1 Digit

Multiply.

	Multiply 3 ones by 2.	Multiply 4 tens by 2.
	43 x 2 **6**	43 x 2 **86**

1.
3	30	2	20	1	10
x 2	x 2	x 2	x 2	x 7	x 7

2.
2	21	3	31	1	11
x 4	x 4	x 3	x 3	x 4	x 4

3.
21	14	22	24	12	34
x 3	x 2	x 3	x 2	x 4	x 2

4.
11	31	33	24	44	23
x 9	x 3	x 3	x 2	x 2	x 2

5.
13	12	23	40	11	14
x 3	x 4	x 2	x 2	x 6	x 2

6.
12	11	21	42	12	13
x 4	x 2	x 3	x 2	x 2	x 3

7.
11	12	20	10	11	40
x 5	x 1	x 4	x 8	x 9	x 2

Practice Page: 2–Digit Multiplication by 1 Digit

Multiply.

	Multiply 2 ones by 3.	Multiply 7 tens by 3.
	72 x 3 **6**	72 x 3 **216**

1.

14	33	12	11	10	21
x 2	x 2	x 3	x 4	x 7	x 3

2.

21	13	71	32	21	52
x 9	x 2	x 5	x 3	x 7	x 2

3.

61	24	31	41	62	60
x 3	x 2	x 3	x 8	x 2	x 5

4.

11	82	33	24	80	44
x 9	x 3	x 3	x 2	x 7	x 2

5.

13	12	23	40	11	14
x 3	x 4	x 2	x 2	x 6	x 2

6.

90	44	51	12	72	80
x 3	x 2	x 4	x 4	x 3	x 4

7.

22	53	90	11	81	42
x 4	x 2	x 2	x 3	x 6	x 3

Practice Page: 2– and 3–Digit Multiplication by 1 Digit

Multiply.

Multiply 4 ones by 3.	Multiply 2 tens by 3. Add the 1 ten.	Multiply 3 hundreds by 3.
1 324 x 3 **2**	1 324 x 3 **72**	1 324 x 3 **972**

1.
45 76 33 85 62 46
x 6 x 3 x 2 x 9 x 5 x 2

2.
59 41 98 75 49 26
x 9 x 5 x 4 x 6 x 4 x 3

3.
76 63 86 48 61 57
x 3 x 3 x 6 x 7 x 2 x 5

4.
58 64 43 93 85 78
x 7 x 6 x 5 x 3 x 8 x 4

5.
98 72 59 48 68 94
x 9 x 4 x 7 x 2 x 7 x 8

6.
84 43 63 84 73 36
x 5 x 7 x 8 x 2 x 3 x 5

7.
267 465 197 286 573 782
x 6 x 4 x 2 x 3 x 9 x 4

Name   Date

Practice Page: 2– and 3–Digit Multiplication by 1 Digit
Multiply.

1.	21 x 5	32 x 3	11 x 8	41 x 2	13 x 2	34 x 2
2.	19 x 2	24 x 3	35 x 2	47 x 2	36 x 4	27 x 4
3.	54 x 4	27 x 6	19 x 6	83 x 7	38 x 4	65 x 4
4.	82 x 9	53 x 7	97 x 2	49 x 4	29 x 8	76 x 5
5.	93 x 5	74 x 6	85 x 7	59 x 3	62 x 6	47 x 4
6.	231 x 2	122 x 3	322 x 2	210 x 4	412 x 2	120 x 3
7.	118 x 3	218 x 2	229 x 4	407 x 2	235 x 3	346 x 2
8.	184 x 2	492 x 2	292 x 4	353 x 2	381 x 4	462 x 3
9.	657 x 4	248 x 6	428 x 5	871 x 3	568 x 7	609 x 4

www.summerbridgeactivities.com   Math Connection—Grade 4—RBP0164

Practice Page: 2– and 3–Digit Multiplication by 1 Digit
Multiply.

1.	31 x 2	22 x 4	11 x 3	31 x 3	11 x 9	20 x 3

1. 31   22   11   31   11   20
    x 2   x 4   x 3   x 3   x 9   x 3

2. 32   13   24   42   11   20
    x 2   x 2   x 2   x 2   x 4   x 7

3. 51   14   27   73   49   16
    x 5   x 7   x 4   x 6   x 3   x 5

4. 35   62   48   83   56   90
    x 4   x 5   x 3   x 6   x 4   x 7

5. 62   92   53   72   80   93
    x 4   x 8   x 6   x 7   x 4   x 5

6. 421   112   204   107   314   211
    x 2   x 3   x 2   x 2   x 2   x 4

7. 215   127   208   419   329   148
    x 3   x 3   x 7   x 2   x 3   x 2

8. 650   581   292   463   381   280
    x 4   x 3   x 4   x 2   x 4   x 7

9. 435   637   384   576   278   457
    x 6   x 8   x 3   x 7   x 5   x 2

Math Connection—Grade 4—RBP0164   www.summerbridgeactivities.com   © RBP Books

Problem Solving: 2– and 3–Digit Multiplication by 1 Digit
Solve each problem.

1.

Jan drove 843 miles. Rex drove 4 times as many miles as Jan. How many miles did Rex drive?

2.

The Blueline express train traveled 5-times farther than the Redline train. The Redline traveled 643 miles. How far did the Blueline train travel?

3.

Jeff drove 249 laps around the race track. If the racetrack is 9 miles long, how many miles did Jeff drive?

4.

The flight from Cedar Junction is 4 times as many miles as the flight from Rapid City. The flight from Rapid City is 789 miles. How far is the flight from Cedar Junction?

5.

Mark traveled 694 miles on his vacation. Susan traveled 3 times as many miles as Mark. How many miles did Susan travel?

6.

Jack drove 129 miles on Monday and 34 miles on Tuesday. If Vicky drove 5 times as many miles as Jack, how many miles did she drive?

7.

If Amanda drove 65 miles per hour, how far did she drive in 7 hours?

8.

Tony drove 543 miles farther than Paul. Paul drove 8 times as many miles as Jeff. If Jeff drove 296 miles, how far did Tony and Paul drive?

www.summerbridgeactivities.com   **Math Connection—Grade 4—RBP0164**

Problem Solving: 2– and 3–Digit Multiplication by 1 Digit

Solve each problem.

1.

Meg and her family are going camping. They travel 329 miles each day. How far do they drive in 4 days to get to the campground?

2.

Luis and his friends hike 15 miles each day. How far do they hike in 4 days?

3.

Batteries in the campers' flashlights last 98 hours. If there are 8 flashlights, how many hours of use will the campers have from their flashlights?

4.

Michelle brought 6 bags of marshmallows to roast. If each bag has 48 marshmallows, how many marshmallows does Michelle have altogether?

5.

At the lake, Amy and her friends paddled in a canoe for 6 hours. If they traveled 183 yards each hour, how far did they travel altogether?

6.

There are 214 campers at each campground. If there are 7 campgrounds, how many campers are there altogether?

7.

Tia is making trail mix to take camping. She makes 152 bags. If each bag holds 9 ounces, how many ounces of trail mix does Tia have altogether?

8.

Casey brings 4 rolls of film with 24 shots on each roll. Antoine brings 7 rolls of film with 36 shots on each roll. How many pictures will Casey and Antoine be able to shoot?

Math Connection—Grade 4—RBP0164   www.summerbridgeactivities.com   ©RBP Books

Post-Test: 2– and 3–Digit Multiplication by 1 Digit

Multiply.

1. $\begin{array}{r}11\\ \times\,5\\\hline\end{array}$	$\begin{array}{r}12\\ \times\,4\\\hline\end{array}$	$\begin{array}{r}21\\ \times\,3\\\hline\end{array}$	$\begin{array}{r}41\\ \times\,2\\\hline\end{array}$	$\begin{array}{r}20\\ \times\,4\\\hline\end{array}$	$\begin{array}{r}31\\ \times\,3\\\hline\end{array}$
2. $\begin{array}{r}24\\ \times\,2\\\hline\end{array}$	$\begin{array}{r}30\\ \times\,3\\\hline\end{array}$	$\begin{array}{r}11\\ \times\,6\\\hline\end{array}$	$\begin{array}{r}23\\ \times\,3\\\hline\end{array}$	$\begin{array}{r}22\\ \times\,4\\\hline\end{array}$	$\begin{array}{r}33\\ \times\,2\\\hline\end{array}$
3. $\begin{array}{r}36\\ \times\,2\\\hline\end{array}$	$\begin{array}{r}29\\ \times\,3\\\hline\end{array}$	$\begin{array}{r}18\\ \times\,6\\\hline\end{array}$	$\begin{array}{r}12\\ \times\,7\\\hline\end{array}$	$\begin{array}{r}26\\ \times\,4\\\hline\end{array}$	$\begin{array}{r}60\\ \times\,4\\\hline\end{array}$
4. $\begin{array}{r}30\\ \times\,7\\\hline\end{array}$	$\begin{array}{r}71\\ \times\,6\\\hline\end{array}$	$\begin{array}{r}63\\ \times\,4\\\hline\end{array}$	$\begin{array}{r}51\\ \times\,3\\\hline\end{array}$	$\begin{array}{r}42\\ \times\,3\\\hline\end{array}$	$\begin{array}{r}39\\ \times\,2\\\hline\end{array}$
5. $\begin{array}{r}57\\ \times\,8\\\hline\end{array}$	$\begin{array}{r}34\\ \times\,7\\\hline\end{array}$	$\begin{array}{r}52\\ \times\,4\\\hline\end{array}$	$\begin{array}{r}64\\ \times\,7\\\hline\end{array}$	$\begin{array}{r}37\\ \times\,6\\\hline\end{array}$	$\begin{array}{r}95\\ \times\,3\\\hline\end{array}$
6. $\begin{array}{r}140\\ \times\,2\\\hline\end{array}$	$\begin{array}{r}230\\ \times\,3\\\hline\end{array}$	$\begin{array}{r}112\\ \times\,4\\\hline\end{array}$	$\begin{array}{r}130\\ \times\,6\\\hline\end{array}$	$\begin{array}{r}428\\ \times\,2\\\hline\end{array}$	$\begin{array}{r}124\\ \times\,3\\\hline\end{array}$
7. $\begin{array}{r}128\\ \times\,4\\\hline\end{array}$	$\begin{array}{r}329\\ \times\,2\\\hline\end{array}$	$\begin{array}{r}424\\ \times\,4\\\hline\end{array}$	$\begin{array}{r}648\\ \times\,2\\\hline\end{array}$	$\begin{array}{r}173\\ \times\,3\\\hline\end{array}$	$\begin{array}{r}391\\ \times\,3\\\hline\end{array}$
8. $\begin{array}{r}658\\ \times\,5\\\hline\end{array}$	$\begin{array}{r}308\\ \times\,3\\\hline\end{array}$	$\begin{array}{r}584\\ \times\,6\\\hline\end{array}$	$\begin{array}{r}279\\ \times\,5\\\hline\end{array}$	$\begin{array}{r}987\\ \times\,3\\\hline\end{array}$	$\begin{array}{r}805\\ \times\,4\\\hline\end{array}$
9. $\begin{array}{r}254\\ \times\,5\\\hline\end{array}$	$\begin{array}{r}661\\ \times\,8\\\hline\end{array}$	$\begin{array}{r}460\\ \times\,7\\\hline\end{array}$	$\begin{array}{r}854\\ \times\,3\\\hline\end{array}$	$\begin{array}{r}726\\ \times\,8\\\hline\end{array}$	$\begin{array}{r}528\\ \times\,4\\\hline\end{array}$

Measurement: Time
Solve each problem.

1. What time will it be in 2 hours and 15 minutes?

2. What time was it 5 hours and 30 minutes earlier?

3. What time was it 3 hours earlier?

4. What time will it be in 3 hours and 45 minutes?

5. What time was it 4 hours and 15 minutes earlier?

6. What time will it be in 1 hour and 30 minutes?

7. What time was it 2 hours and 30 minutes earlier?

8. What time will it be in 6 hours and 15 minutes?

Solve each problem.

9. Ryan left 25 minutes before his soccer lesson. If his soccer lesson was at 2:45 P.M., what time did Ryan leave?

10. Terry has 50 minutes left to shop before the mall closes. It is 9:05 P.M. What time does the mall close?

11. Amber arrived 25 minutes early for her dentist appointment. If her appointment was scheduled for 7:45 A.M., what time did Amber arrive at the dentist's office?

12. Cassie left the movie at 9:15 P.M. She stopped for 30 minutes to eat dinner. Then she drove home in 15 minutes. What time did Cassie get home?

Pre-Test: 2– and 3–Digit Multiplication by 2 Digits

Multiply.

1.	21	34	17	62	43	75
	x 30	x 20	x 50	x 20	x 60	x 30

2.	31	16	25	36	73	28
	x 26	x 21	x 13	x 23	x 42	x 42

Multiply.

3.	203	480	901	560	110	740
	x 27	x 31	x 74	x 19	x 56	x 64

4.	531	124	618	492	314	764
	x 34	x 72	x 24	x 61	x 83	x 19

5.	364	861	365	415	637	208
	x 41	x 40	x 32	x 57	x 18	x 45

Practice Page: 2– and 3–Digit Multiplication by 2 Digits
Multiply.

	If …	Then …
	12 x 2 24	12 x 20 **240**

Whoa! I'm multiplying!

1.

12	12	26	26	42	42
x 2	x 20	x 4	x 40	x 3	x 30

2.

16	16	36	36	23	23
x 3	x 30	x 3	x 30	x 5	x 50

3.

31	31	16	16	41	41
x 4	x 40	x 4	x 40	x 5	x 50

4.

62	62	27	27	42	42
x 4	x 40	x 9	x 90	x 1	x 10

Math Connection—Grade 4—RBP0164   www.summerbridgeactivities.com   © RBP Books

Name _____   Date _____

Practice Page: 2– and 3–Digit Multiplication by 2 Digits
Multiply.

	Multiply 12 by 2 ones.	Multiply 12 by 3 tens.	Add.
12 x 32	12 x 32 24	12 x 32 24 360	12 x 32 24 + 360 **384**

1.

| 14
x 2 | 14
x 20 | 27
x 4 | 27
x 40 | 45
x 3 | 45
x 30 |

2.

| 24
x 3 | 24
x 43 | 19
x 3 | 19
x 23 | 18
x 5 | 18
x 15 |

3.

| 62
x 3 | 62
x 43 | 57
x 9 | 57
x 19 | 27
x 5 | 27
x 45 |

4.

| 81
x 7 | 81
x 37 | 32
x 5 | 32
x 65 | 94
x 6 | 94
x 26 |

www.summerbridgeactivities.com   **Math Connection—Grade 4—RBP0164**

Practice Page: 2– and 3–Digit Multiplication by 2 Digits

Multiply.

1.
37	37	64	64	24	24
x 2	x 12	x 4	x 34	x 3	x 83

2.
13	24	24	18	34	43
x 24	x 32	x 11	x 23	x 52	x 24

3.
34	41	15	34	53	17
x 12	x 31	x 23	x 21	x 13	x 12

4.
42	14	25	17	35	26
x 31	x 25	x 32	x 21	x 11	x 13

5.
30	17	84	67	53	19
x 29	x 64	x 50	x 15	x 41	x 63

Practice Page: 2– and 3–Digit Multiplication by 2 Digits

Multiply.

	Multiply 45 by 9 ones.	Multiply 45 by 2 tens.	Add.
45 x 29	$\overset{4}{4}5$ x 29 405	$\overset{1}{4}5$ x 29 405 900	45 x 29 405 + 900 **1,305**

1.   51   76   39   78   96   62
     x 30   x 40   x 20   x 40   x 70   x 60

2.   23   34   11   23   33   13
     x 42   x 12   x 43   x 32   x 41   x 45

3.   28   47   87   58   63   76
     x 36   x 62   x 29   x 34   x 19   x 38

4.   15   93   18   49   18   67
     x 87   x 62   x 34   x 52   x 64   x 69

Name _____   Date _____

Practice Page: 2– and 3–Digit Multiplication by 2 Digits

Multiply.

1.
$$\begin{array}{r} 64 \\ \times\,20 \\ \hline \end{array}$$
$$\begin{array}{r} 37 \\ \times\,10 \\ \hline \end{array}$$
$$\begin{array}{r} 56 \\ \times\,80 \\ \hline \end{array}$$
$$\begin{array}{r} 19 \\ \times\,30 \\ \hline \end{array}$$
$$\begin{array}{r} 87 \\ \times\,50 \\ \hline \end{array}$$
$$\begin{array}{r} 92 \\ \times\,70 \\ \hline \end{array}$$

2.
$$\begin{array}{r} 18 \\ \times\,25 \\ \hline \end{array}$$
$$\begin{array}{r} 64 \\ \times\,31 \\ \hline \end{array}$$
$$\begin{array}{r} 53 \\ \times\,12 \\ \hline \end{array}$$
$$\begin{array}{r} 23 \\ \times\,62 \\ \hline \end{array}$$
$$\begin{array}{r} 46 \\ \times\,30 \\ \hline \end{array}$$
$$\begin{array}{r} 19 \\ \times\,32 \\ \hline \end{array}$$

3.
$$\begin{array}{r} 62 \\ \times\,21 \\ \hline \end{array}$$
$$\begin{array}{r} 27 \\ \times\,84 \\ \hline \end{array}$$
$$\begin{array}{r} 49 \\ \times\,67 \\ \hline \end{array}$$
$$\begin{array}{r} 36 \\ \times\,25 \\ \hline \end{array}$$
$$\begin{array}{r} 57 \\ \times\,26 \\ \hline \end{array}$$
$$\begin{array}{r} 37 \\ \times\,18 \\ \hline \end{array}$$

4.
$$\begin{array}{r} 92 \\ \times\,16 \\ \hline \end{array}$$
$$\begin{array}{r} 31 \\ \times\,28 \\ \hline \end{array}$$
$$\begin{array}{r} 19 \\ \times\,66 \\ \hline \end{array}$$
$$\begin{array}{r} 21 \\ \times\,82 \\ \hline \end{array}$$
$$\begin{array}{r} 62 \\ \times\,83 \\ \hline \end{array}$$
$$\begin{array}{r} 19 \\ \times\,43 \\ \hline \end{array}$$

5.
$$\begin{array}{r} 81 \\ \times\,15 \\ \hline \end{array}$$
$$\begin{array}{r} 57 \\ \times\,33 \\ \hline \end{array}$$
$$\begin{array}{r} 12 \\ \times\,85 \\ \hline \end{array}$$
$$\begin{array}{r} 76 \\ \times\,19 \\ \hline \end{array}$$
$$\begin{array}{r} 69 \\ \times\,73 \\ \hline \end{array}$$
$$\begin{array}{r} 86 \\ \times\,79 \\ \hline \end{array}$$

Math Connection—Grade 4—RBP0164   www.summerbridgeactivities.com   ©RBP Books

Practice Page: 2– and 3–Digit Multiplication by 2 Digits

Multiply.

	Multiply 612 by 7 ones.	Multiply 612 by 3 tens.	Add.
612 x 37	$\overset{1}{612}$ x 37 4,284	612 x 37 4,284 18,360	612 x 37 4,284 + 18,360 **22,644**

1.

219 x 2	219 x 20	511 x 4	511 x 40	362 x 7	362 x 70

2.

125 x 2	125 x 12	324 x 5	324 x 35	251 x 5	251 x 45

3.

127 x 32	461 x 63	214 x 28	513 x 41	614 x 16

4.

324 x 19	635 x 54	431 x 35	723 x 27	285 x 45

Practice Page: 2– and 3–Digit Multiplication by 2 Digits

Multiply.

1.	541 x 3	541 x 30	219 x 2	219 x 20	643 x 6	643 x 60

2.	457 x 2	457 x 32	267 x 3	267 x 43	815 x 5	815 x 65

3.	365 x 19	221 x 54	649 x 36	379 x 22	453 x 21

4.	953 x 43	627 x 24	419 x 82	591 x 36	849 x 72

5.	247 x 63	244 x 49	821 x 53	776 x 67	132 x 98

Math Connection—Grade 4—RBP0164   www.summerbridgeactivities.com   © RBP Books

Name _____   Date _____

Practice Page: 2– and 3–Digit Multiplication by 2 Digits
Multply.

1.
| 62 | 36 | 57 | 81 | 29 | 63 |
| x 12 | x 40 | x 32 | x 47 | x 76 | x 81 |

2.
| 26 | 65 | 54 | 92 | 48 | 84 |
| x 78 | x 49 | x 37 | x 26 | x 54 | x 39 |

3.
| 51 | 39 | 78 | 18 | 43 | 65 |
| x 47 | x 72 | x 29 | x 34 | x 19 | x 52 |

4.
| 246 | 613 | 443 | 921 | 509 |
| x 43 | x 24 | x 57 | x 38 | x 76 |

5.
| 429 | 861 | 697 | 348 | 958 |
| x 16 | x 76 | x 23 | x 28 | x 82 |

Practice Page: 2– and 3–Digit Multiplication by 2 Digits
Multiply.

1. 19	83	24	59	38	12
x 40	x 23	x 62	x 73	x 65	x 53

2. 89	26	31	79	94	52
x 60	x 47	x 18	x 26	x 31	x 39

3. 672	951	355	241	894	453
x 18	x 46	x 71	x 65	x 70	x 57

4. 120	381	214	591	691	709
x 94	x 47	x 38	x 77	x 84	x 47

5. 475	595	910	317	683	209
x 59	x 42	x 65	x 29	x 15	x 68

Math Connection—Grade 4—RBP0164   www.summerbridgeactivities.com   ©RBP Books

Problem Solving: 2– and 3– Digit Multiplication by 2 Digits

Solve each problem.

1.

The Cruisin' Coaster has 19 cars. If 37 people can ride in each car, how many people can ride at the same time?

2.

At the sweet shop, 833 people bought cotton candy. If cotton candy costs $0.57, how much did the sweet shop earn?

3.

The bumper cars run 148 times during the day. If 39 people can ride each time the cars run, how many people can ride the bumper cars during the day?

4.

One trip around the park in the train is 18 miles long. If the train went around the park 294 times during the day, how many miles did it travel?

5.

The Jungle Adventure boats hold 14 people. If there are 24 boats, how many people can ride at the same time?

6.

The Lots-of-Fun park charges $39 for an all-day pass to the park. If 842 people visited the park, how much money did the park make?

7.

Amy sold 48 sodas. If each soda costs $1.29, how much money did Amy earn?

8.

Hank and his friends waited 15 minutes in line for each ride. If they rode 38 rides, how many minutes did they spend waiting in line?

www.summerbridgeactivities.com

Math Connection—Grade 4—RBP0164

Problem Solving: 2– and 3–Digit Multiplication by 2 Digits
Solve each problem.

1. Erica has 147 raspberry bushes. Each bush has 29 raspberries. How many raspberries does Erica have altogether?

2. Corey has 24 packages of sunflower seeds. If each package has 15 seeds, how many sunflower seeds does he have altogether?

3. Monica's yard measures 63 feet by 94 feet. How many square feet does she need to buy fertilizer for?

4. Allison is cleaning up her yard. She has 18 boxes of trash bags. If each box has 25 trash bags, how many trash bags does she have altogether?

5. Mike mows a lawn that is 107 feet by 83 feet. How many square feet of lawn does Mike mow?

6. Jamal planted 47 plants on each row in his garden. If Jamal's garden has 15 rows, how many plants does he have?

7. Anita has 216 peach trees in her orchard. If she picks 22 peaches from each tree, how many peaches does she pick?

8. Marie has 19 marigold plants. Each plant has 11 flowers. She also has 35 daisy plants. Each daisy plant has 17 flowers. How many flowers does she have altogether?

Post-Test: 2– and 3–Digit Multiplication by 2 Digits
Multiply.

1.	29 x 30	54 x 50	19 x 20	62 x 70	87 x 60
2.	31 x 43	13 x 26	36 x 54	63 x 71	41 x 25
3.	62 x 41	16 x 37	83 x 29	67 x 29	53 x 48
4.	257 x 96	381 x 28	681 x 42	537 x 57	792 x 34
5.	964 x 26	627 x 49	176 x 87	804 x 54	227 x 39

Number Patterns

Read the number rule on each balloon. Fill in the missing numbers.

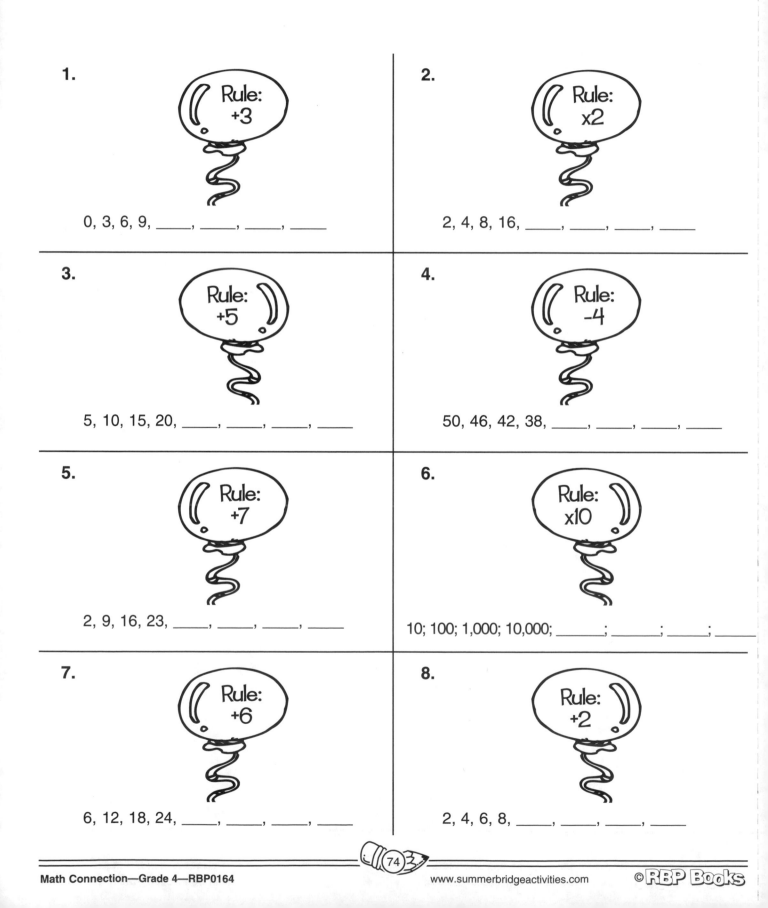

1.

Rule:
+3

0, 3, 6, 9, _____, _____, _____, _____

2.

Rule:
x2

2, 4, 8, 16, _____, _____, _____, _____

3.

Rule:
+5

5, 10, 15, 20, _____, _____, _____, _____

4.

Rule:
-4

50, 46, 42, 38, _____, _____, _____, _____

5.

Rule:
+7

2, 9, 16, 23, _____, _____, _____, _____

6.

Rule:
x10

10; 100; 1,000; 10,000; _____; _____; _____; _____

7.

Rule:
+6

6, 12, 18, 24, _____, _____, _____, _____

8.

Rule:
+2

2, 4, 6, 8, _____, _____, _____, _____

Pre-Test: 4–Digit Multiplication by 1, 2, 3, and 4 Digits

Multiply.

1.

2,143	1,032	5,174	3,264
x 2	x 4	x 7	x 5

2.

3,971	2,354	5,917	8,412
x 43	x 61	x 72	x 83

3.

671	306	527	768
x 917	x 294	x 411	x 248

4.

8,191	6,517	3,271	6,907
x 324	x 517	x 481	x 823

5.

6,172	5,064	2,581	6,340
x 2,341	x 3,624	x 2,214	x 2,154

Practice Page: 4–Digit Multiplication by 1 Digit

Multiply.

| 5,129
x   2 | Multiply 9 ones by 2.
$\overset{1}{5,129}$
x   2
8 | Multiply 2 tens by 2.
Remember to add the 1.
$\overset{1}{5,129}$
x   2
58 | Multiply 1 hundred by 2.
5,129
x   2
258 | Multiply 5 thousands by 2.
5,129
x   2
10,258 |

1.

| 2,000
x   3 | 3,000
x   3 | 2,110
x   4 | 3,021
x   2 | 4,210
x   3 |

2.

| 3,145
x   2 | 2,041
x   4 | 5,120
x   6 | 6,814
x   2 | 8,521
x   3 |

3.

| 6,271
x   4 | 8,432
x   7 | 5,179
x   2 | 9,034
x   5 | 3,679
x   4 |

4.

| 3,241
x   3 | 2,324
x   6 | 8,971
x   4 | 4,809
x   2 | 9,834
x   7 |

5.

| 8,412
x   2 | 9,635
x   4 | 6,716
x   5 | 3,679
x   6 | 2,647
x   8 |

Math Connection—Grade 4—RBP0164   www.summerbridgeactivities.com   ©RBP Books

Practice Page: 4–Digit Multiplication by 2, 3, and 4 Digits

Multiply.

	Multiply 1,249 by 2 ones.	Multiply 1,249 by 3 tens.	Add.
1,249 x 32	¹ 1,249 x 32 2,498	¹² 1,249 x 32 2,498 37,470	1,249 x 32 2,498 + 37,470 **39,968**

1.
3,000   3,000   6,000   6,000
x   2   x 20   x   6   x 60

2.
5,000   6,000   7,000   8,000
x 30   x 40   x 30   x 40

3.
3,028   5,413   2,135   4,361
x 41   x 23   x 16   x 34

4.
6,179   1,349   4,564   5,347
x 82   x 64   x 41   x 35

5.
9,187   6,481   7,492   8,049
x 54   x 62   x 37   x 12

Practice Page: 4–Digit Multiplication by 2 Digits

1.	3,601 x 15	5,015 x 21	1,264 x 25	2,641 x 41
2.	3,216 x 47	2,643 x 39	3,180 x 13	8,436 x 42
3.	1,345 x 62	3,406 x 21	5,348 x 51	2,648 x 18
4.	9,018 x 54	2,667 x 36	1,064 x 28	6,912 x 46
5.	8,043 x 12	3,642 x 51	6,057 x 43	5,803 x 86

Math Connection—Grade 4—RBP0164 www.summerbridgeactivities.com ©RBP Books

Practice Page: 4–Digit Multiplication by 3 Digits
Multiply.

214 x 642	Multiply 214 by 2.	Multiply 214 by 4 tens.	Multiply 214 by 6 hundreds.	Add.
	214 x 642 428	$\overset{1}{2}14$ x 642 428 8,560	$\overset{2}{2}14$ x 642 428 8,560 128,400	214 x 642 428 8,560 + 128,400 **137,388**

1.

116 x 200	262 x 300	624 x 700	561 x 400

2.

513 x 124	216 x 320	321 x 124	262 x 414

3.

206 x 417	354 x 124	513 x 216	618 x 407

4.

2,134 x 312	1,345 x 113	5,614 x 621	3,246 x 207

5.

6,171 x 429	4,913 x 162	3,164 x 204	5,132 x 324

Practice Page: 4–Digit Multiplication by 2, 3, and 4 Digits

Multiply.

1.
3,215	2,013	4,613	6,241
x 14	x 34	x 11	x 42

2.
1,946	8,132	1,805	6,241
x 32	x 46	x 24	x 35

3.
2,156	5,164	7,018	3,612
x 324	x 352	x 149	x 804

4.
7,482	2,151	9,081	7,616
x 2,134	x 1,252	x 1,251	x 3,104

Math Connection—Grade 4—RBP0164   www.summerbridgeactivities.com   ©RBP Books

Problem Solving: 4–Digit Multiplication by 2, 3, and 4 Digits

Figure out the number of pages each book club member read. Make a table to help organize the information.

Caroline read 23 times as many pages as Max.

Julie read 346 pages more than Greg.

Max read half as many pages as Allison.

Greg read 1,598 pages fewer than Caroline.

Allison read 2,424 pages.

Becky read 32 times as many pages as Greg.

Jeff read 15 times as many pages as Allison.

Name	Pages Read

Problem Solving: 4–Digit Multiplication by 2, 3, and 4 Digits

Solve each problem.

1.

Marcy and her friends are planning a carnival. They are planning on 3,389 people for each day. If the carnival is open for 5 days, how many people should they plan for altogether?

2.

Sidney buys prizes for the Toss-a-Ring game. She buys 15 times as many rubber balls as toy cars. If she buys 1,382 toy cars, how many rubber balls does she buy?

3.

Marcy sells 1,065 gallons of orange punch. She sells 24 times as many gallons of red punch as orange punch. How many gallons of red punch does Marcy sell?

4.

Andy buys 2,959 tickets for 25¢ each. What is the total amount Andy spends?

5.

Ricky has 3,473 T-shirts made to sell at the carnival. He only sells 2,088 T-shirts. If he charges $5.75 for each T-shirt, how much money does he earn altogether?

6.

On Monday, 2,476 people go to the carnival. The same number of people go to the carnival on Tuesday and on Wednesday. How many people go to the carnival altogether?

7.

Isabella buys 4,832 pints of chocolate ice cream. If Isabella buys 28 times as many pints of vanilla ice cream as chocolate ice cream, how many pints of vanilla ice cream does she buy?

8.

Tyler buys 2,388 red balloons. He buys 7 times as many blue balloons as red balloons. Then, he buys 12 times as many yellow balloons as blue balloons. How many balloons does Tyler buy altogether?

Post-Test: 4–Digit Multiplication by 1, 2, 3, and 4 Digits
Multiply.

1. 3,115   6,302   9,172   5,126
    x   3   x   6   x   2   x   5

2. 3,691   5,126   2,691   6,015
    x 21   x 13   x 84   x 49

3.   315   761   612   237
    x 429   x 112   x 549   x 840

4. 6,412   5,925   2,618   8,205
    x 214   x 413   x 119   x 561

5. 1,257   2,147   2,181   7,112
    x 1,602   x 3,719   x 1,721   x 4,091

Money

Write the decimal numbers for the amounts below.

1. 6 dollars and 35 cents = $ _____

2. 9 dollars and 27 cents = $ _____

3. 4 dollars and 42 cents = $ _____

4. 5 dollars and 75 cents = $ _____

5. 7 dollars and 61 cents = $ _____

6. 3 dollars and 84 cents = $ _____

Write the decimal numbers for the amounts below.

7. Fifteen dollars and twenty-two cents = $ _____

8. Twenty-four dollars and thirty-four cents = $ _____

9. Fifty-seven dollars and nineteen cents = $ _____

10. Seventy dollars and ninety-nine cents = $ _____

11. Thirty-five dollars and twenty-nine cents = $ _____

12. Eighty-five dollars and fifteen cents = $ _____

Answer each question.

13.
What is the total value of 3 quarters and 5 nickels?

14.
What is the total value of 9 dimes, 2 nickels, and 7 pennies?

15.
What is the total value of 4 one-dollar bills, 3 quarters, 4 dimes, and 2 pennies?

16.
What is the total value of 3 five-dollar bills, 4 dimes, 1 nickel, and 8 pennies?

17.
What is the total value of 6 ten-dollar bills, 5 dimes, 1 nickel, and 7 pennies?

18.
What is the total value of 5 quarters, 2 dimes, and 1 nickel?

Math Connection—Grade 4—RBP0164
www.summerbridgeactivities.com

Money
Add or Subtract.

Add the **ones** column.	Add the **tens** column.	Add the **hundreds** column.	Write the **decimal point** and **dollar sign** in your answer.
$\overset{1}{\$1.29}$ $+\ 6.55$ $\overline{4}$	$\overset{1}{\$1.29}$ $+\ 6.55$ $\overline{84}$	$\overset{1}{\$1.29}$ $+\ 6.55$ $\overline{7\ 84}$	$\overset{1}{\$1.29}$ $+\ 6.55$ $\overline{\mathbf{\$7.84}}$

1.
$\$0.45$ $+\ 0.56$	$\$0.19$ $+\ 0.27$	$\$0.16$ $+\ 0.30$	$\$0.65$ $-\ 0.17$	$\$0.86$ $-\ 0.44$

2.
$\$9.65$ $-\ 0.46$	$\$7.87$ $+\ 0.40$	$\$1.35$ $+\ 0.15$	$\$2.29$ $-\ 0.75$	$\$8.65$ $+\ 0.24$

3.
$\$5.24$ $+\ 0.64$	$\$6.12$ $+\ 0.98$	$\$4.55$ $+\ 0.55$	$\$1.65$ $-\ 0.25$	$\$9.05$ $-\ 0.49$

4.
$\$7.00$ $+\ 0.65$	$\$8.84$ $-\ 0.29$	$\$6.87$ $+\ 0.85$	$\$9.36$ $+\ 0.95$	$\$3.00$ $-\ 0.45$

5.
$\$5.00$ $+\ 3.87$	$\$9.61$ $-\ 1.62$	$\$1.30$ $-\ 0.25$	$\$7.00$ $-\ 2.95$	$\$2.49$ $+\ 6.17$

6.
$\$42.00$ $+\ 54.86$	$\$64.75$ $-\ 34.09$	$\$19.66$ $-\ 11.49$	$\$37.16$ $-\ 18.15$	$\$87.55$ $+\ 29.65$

Money

$0.45 x 23	Multiply 45 by 3 **ones**.	Multiply 45 by 2 **tens**.	Add.	Count the number of decimal places and write the decimal point and $ sign in your answer.
	$\overset{1}{\$0.45}$ x 23 135	$\overset{1}{\$0.45}$ x 23 135 900	$0.45 x 23 135 + 900 1,035	$0.45 x 23 135 + 900 **$10.35**

Multiply.

1. $0.65 $0.40 $1.57 $19.95 $81.79
    x   2   x   7   x   3   x   4   x   5

2. $0.24 $0.90 $0.18 $4.25 $2.19
    x 16   x 62   x 75   x 23   x 55

3. $19.61 $1.55 $4.65 $81.49 $16.75
    x 212   x 110   x 308   x 322   x 551

Answer each question.

4. Alex bought 6 baseball cards for $1.25 each. How much did he spend?

5. Apples are $0.79 a pound. Marcy bought 8 pounds. How much did she spend?

6. Jamie bought 7 bags of peanuts for $2.49 per bag. How much did she spend on peanuts?

7. Marissa bought 15 tickets for $34.49 each. How much did she spend?

Pre-Test: Division
Divide.

1. $9\overline{)72}$ $6\overline{)12}$ $8\overline{)40}$ $2\overline{)4}$ $4\overline{)28}$

2. $5\overline{)20}$ $9\overline{)0}$ $6\overline{)6}$ $7\overline{)35}$ $8\overline{)72}$

3. $9\overline{)27}$ $7\overline{)56}$ $3\overline{)27}$ $2\overline{)14}$ $3\overline{)18}$

4. $1\overline{)6}$ $4\overline{)16}$ $8\overline{)48}$ $6\overline{)42}$ $9\overline{)36}$

5. $9\overline{)81}$ $7\overline{)14}$ $4\overline{)36}$ $8\overline{)40}$ $7\overline{)63}$

6. $2\overline{)10}$ $6\overline{)48}$ $1\overline{)7}$ $5\overline{)40}$ $8\overline{)16}$

7. $8\overline{)24}$ $4\overline{)4}$ $5\overline{)45}$ $8\overline{)56}$ $2\overline{)18}$

8. $6\overline{)36}$ $3\overline{)21}$ $8\overline{)32}$ $9\overline{)18}$ $6\overline{)18}$

9. $5\overline{)30}$ $9\overline{)63}$ $4\overline{)32}$ $3\overline{)24}$ $7\overline{)42}$

10. $9\overline{)54}$ $5\overline{)0}$ $9\overline{)9}$ $7\overline{)28}$ $9\overline{)45}$

Practice Page: Division

	If …	Then …
	2 x 3 = 6	$3\overline{)6}$ = **2**
	3 x 2 = 6	$2\overline{)6}$ = **3**

1. 3 x 2 = 6   3 x 3 = 9   2 x 4 = 8   7 x 1 = 7
$2\overline{)6}$ = ____ $3\overline{)9}$ = ____ $4\overline{)8}$ = ____ $1\overline{)7}$ = ____

2. 5 x 0 = 0   4 x 5 = 20   6 x 3 = 18   4 x 3 = 12
$5\overline{)0}$ = ____ $4\overline{)20}$ = ____ $3\overline{)18}$ = ____ $4\overline{)12}$ = ____

3. 6 x 6 = 36   2 x 5 = 10   2 x 7 = 14   4 x 9 = 36
$6\overline{)36}$ = ____ $2\overline{)10}$ = ____ $7\overline{)14}$ = ____ $4\overline{)36}$ = ____

4. 7 x 3 = 21   6 x 8 = 48   5 x 5 = 25   9 x 7 = 63
$7\overline{)21}$ = ____ $6\overline{)48}$ = ____ $5\overline{)25}$ = ____ $9\overline{)63}$ = ____

5. 4 x 8 = 32   4 x 6 = 24   8 x 7 = 56   2 x 8 = 16
$8\overline{)32}$ = ____ $6\overline{)24}$ = ____ $8\overline{)56}$ = ____ $2\overline{)16}$ = ____

6. 9 x 2 = 18   7 x 7 = 49   3 x 8 = 24   6 x 7 = 42
$9\overline{)18}$ = ____ $7\overline{)49}$ = ____ $8\overline{)24}$ = ____ $7\overline{)42}$ = ____

7. 4 x 4 = 16   5 x 3 = 15   4 x 7 = 28   8 x 8 = 64
$4\overline{)16}$ = ____ $3\overline{)15}$ = ____ $7\overline{)28}$ = ____ $8\overline{)64}$ = ____

Name _____   Date _____

Practice Page: Division

	If …	Then …
	$3 \times 5 = 15$	$5\overline{)15} = 3$
	$5 \times 3 = 15$	$3\overline{)15} = 5$

1. $9 \times 3 = 27$ $5 \times 2 = 10$ $4 \times 3 = 12$ $8 \times 3 = 24$

$3\overline{)27} = \underline{\hphantom{00}}$ $2\overline{)10} = \underline{\hphantom{00}}$ $3\overline{)12} = \underline{\hphantom{00}}$ $3\overline{)24} = \underline{\hphantom{00}}$

2. $9 \times 7 = 63$ $4 \times 5 = 20$ $8 \times 6 = 48$ $5 \times 1 = 5$

$7\overline{)63} = \underline{\hphantom{00}}$ $5\overline{)20} = \underline{\hphantom{00}}$ $6\overline{)48} = \underline{\hphantom{00}}$ $1\overline{)5} = \underline{\hphantom{00}}$

3. $6 \times 6 = 36$ $8 \times 2 = 16$ $7 \times 5 = 35$ $7 \times 8 = 56$

$6\overline{)36} = \underline{\hphantom{00}}$ $2\overline{)16} = \underline{\hphantom{00}}$ $5\overline{)35} = \underline{\hphantom{00}}$ $8\overline{)56} = \underline{\hphantom{00}}$

4. $9 \times 6 = 54$ $5 \times 6 = 30$ $9 \times 8 = 72$ $7 \times 3 = 21$

$6\overline{)54} = \underline{\hphantom{00}}$ $6\overline{)30} = \underline{\hphantom{00}}$ $8\overline{)72} = \underline{\hphantom{00}}$ $3\overline{)21} = \underline{\hphantom{00}}$

Divide.

5. $9\overline{)36}^{\,4}$ $4\overline{)16}$ $8\overline{)0}$ $5\overline{)40}$ $9\overline{)18}$

6. $2\overline{)14}$ $9\overline{)81}$ $7\overline{)56}$ $1\overline{)4}$ $7\overline{)63}$

7. $8\overline{)32}$ $6\overline{)42}$ $2\overline{)16}$ $8\overline{)48}$ $3\overline{)9}$

    www.summerbridgeactivities.com   **Math Connection—Grade 4—RBP0164**

Practice Page: Division

1. $7 \times 4 = 28$ $6 \times 6 = 36$ $2 \times 8 = 16$ $7 \times 3 = 21$
   $4\overline{)28} = \underline{\quad}$ $6\overline{)36} = \underline{\quad}$ $8\overline{)16} = \underline{\quad}$ $3\overline{)21} = \underline{\quad}$

2. $8 \times 1 = 8$ $3 \times 8 = 24$ $4 \times 4 = 16$ $8 \times 5 = 40$
   $1\overline{)8} = \underline{\quad}$ $8\overline{)24} = \underline{\quad}$ $4\overline{)16} = \underline{\quad}$ $5\overline{)40} = \underline{\quad}$

3. $7 \times 6 = 42$ $7 \times 5 = 35$ $6 \times 3 = 18$ $0 \times 9 = 0$
   $6\overline{)42} = \underline{\quad}$ $5\overline{)35} = \underline{\quad}$ $3\overline{)18} = \underline{\quad}$ $9\overline{)0} = \underline{\quad}$

4. $6 \times 4 = 24$ $8 \times 9 = 72$ $6 \times 2 = 12$ $5 \times 5 = 25$
   $4\overline{)24} = \underline{\quad}$ $9\overline{)72} = \underline{\quad}$ $2\overline{)12} = \underline{\quad}$ $5\overline{)25} = \underline{\quad}$

Divide.

5. $2\overline{)12}$ $9\overline{)72}$ $7\overline{)49}$ $1\overline{)3}$ $7\overline{)56}$

6. $8\overline{)40}$ $6\overline{)48}$ $2\overline{)18}$ $8\overline{)56}$ $3\overline{)12}$

7. $7\overline{)35}$ $9\overline{)36}$ $6\overline{)0}$ $6\overline{)30}$ $6\overline{)12}$

8. $8\overline{)72}$ $9\overline{)54}$ $7\overline{)21}$ $6\overline{)12}$ $8\overline{)16}$

Problem Solving: Division

Solve each problem.

1.

Kayla has 24 sheets of colored paper. If there are 6 students, how many sheets of paper will each student get?

2.

Craig has $12. He buys bottles of glue for $2 each. How many bottles of glue can Craig buy?

3.

There are 30 people in Russ's class. Russ buys one eraser for each of the students. Erasers are sold 5 to a package. How many packages of erasers does Russ need to buy?

4.

Denise buys 63 rulers for her class. How many boxes of rulers does Denise buy if each box contains 9 rulers?

5.

Marcus needs to buy notebooks for 48 students in his class. If each carton contains 8 notebooks, how many cartons does Marcus need to buy to give one to each student?

6.

Jasmine brings candy for the class. If there are 72 students in her class, and each package of candy has 9 pieces, how many packages of candy does Jasmine need to bring to give each student one piece?

7.

Sam shares stickers with his class. There are 4 stickers on a sheet. If there are 28 people in Sam's class, how many sheets of stickers does Sam need to give each person one sticker?

8.

Chloe has $15 to spend on pencils. Each box of pencils costs $2. How many boxes of pencils can Chloe buy? How much money does Chloe have left after she buys the pencils?

Problem Solving: Division
Solve each problem.

1.
Alice buys 54 cookies. If there are 6 cookies in each package, how many packages of cookies does she buy?

2.
Doris buys 60 eggs. How many cartons of eggs does she buy if there are 12 eggs in 1 carton?

3.
Matt spends $28 at the grocery store. If he buys 7 boxes of Tasty-Oaties, how much does each box of cereal cost him?

4.
Robin spent $66 on 6 jumbo cans of soup. How much did each can cost?

5.
Alexis needs 60 paper plates. If there are 9 paper plates in 1 package, how many packages of paper plates should Alexis buy? How many extra paper plates will she have?

6.
Gary buys 40 ounces of punch. If each bottle holds 8 ounces of punch, how many bottles does Gary buy?

7.
Stephanie buys 44 potatoes. How many bags of potatoes does Stephanie buy if there are 11 potatoes in 1 bag?

8.
Caroline has $24 to spend on meat. The meat costs $3 per pound. How many pounds of meat can Caroline buy?

Name _____ Date _____

Post-Test: Division
Divide.

The digits are really coming down today!

1. 6)48 9)45 6)24 3)24 6)54

2. 3)12 3)21 4)4 5)45 5)30

3. 8)40 2)14 8)72 6)18 7)42

4. 5)0 7)63 2)4 3)27 8)32

5. 8)48 9)27 7)21 9)18 6)42

6. 6)0 1)7 9)36 6)12 7)56

7. 5)40 8)16 4)16 7)28 9)81

8. 8)8 2)18 9)63 5)20 9)72

9.
Sarah buys 35 gumdrops. She gives 5 friends the same number of gumdrops. How many gumdrops does each friend get?

10.
Meg is packaging chocolates. She has 56 chocolates and 7 boxes. If she puts the same number of chocolates in each box, how many chocolates will each box have?

Name _____   Date _____

Measurement: Reading a Thermometer
Write the temperature showing on the thermometer in the space below.

Temperatures are measured in Fahrenheit (F) and Celsius (C). 32 degrees Fahrenheit is equal to 0 degrees Celsius.

1.

_____ **75°** _____ F   _____ F   _____ F

2.

_____ C   _____ C   _____ C

3.

_____ F   _____ F   _____ F

4.

_____ C   _____ C   _____ C

Math Connection—Grade 4—RBP0164   www.summerbridgeactivities.com   © RBP Books

Pre-Test: 2– and 3–Digit Division with and without Remainders

Divide.

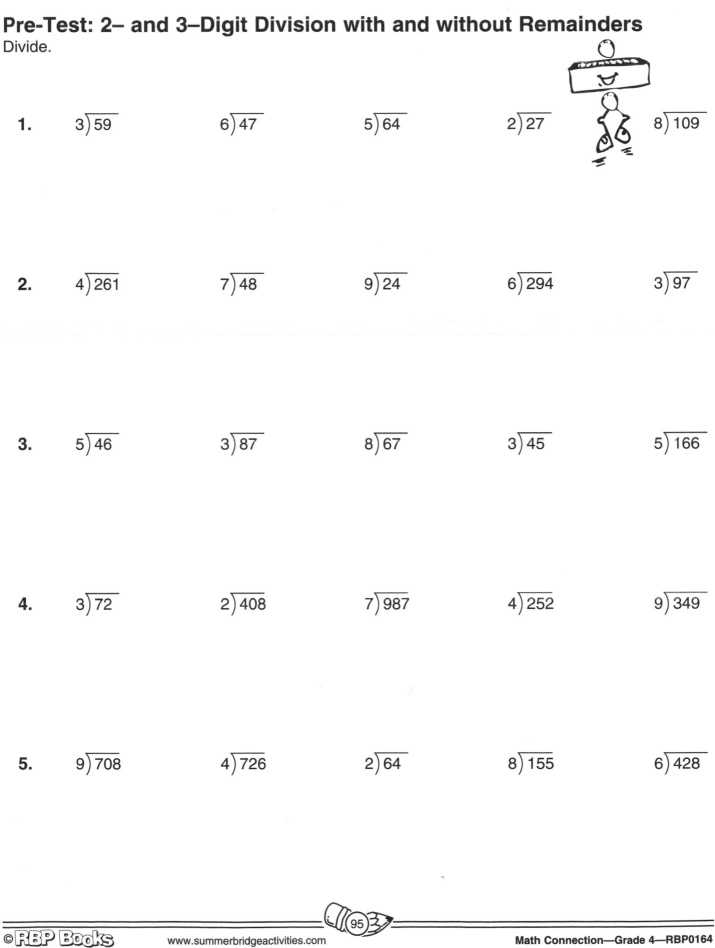

1. 3)59   6)47   5)64   2)27   8)109

2. 4)261   7)48   9)24   6)294   3)97

3. 5)46   3)87   8)67   3)45   5)166

4. 3)72   2)408   7)987   4)252   9)349

5. 9)708   4)726   2)64   8)155   6)428

Practice Page: 2–Digit Division without Remainders
Divide.

$$\begin{array}{r} \mathbf{16}\ \mathbf{R1} \\ 2\overline{)33} \\ \underline{-2} \\ 13 \\ \underline{-12} \\ 1 \end{array}$$

2 x 1 = 2 Subtract 2 from 3.

2 x 6 = 12 Subtract 12 from 13.
Because 13 − 12 = 1, there is a remainder of 1.

1. $3\overline{)42}$ $2\overline{)26}$ $4\overline{)84}$ $7\overline{)56}$ $8\overline{)88}$

2. $2\overline{)24}$ $5\overline{)50}$ $3\overline{)36}$ $4\overline{)48}$ $4\overline{)52}$

3. $5\overline{)70}$ $6\overline{)84}$ $2\overline{)32}$ $3\overline{)42}$ $7\overline{)98}$

4. $4\overline{)60}$ $7\overline{)91}$ $6\overline{)78}$ $8\overline{)80}$ $5\overline{)75}$

5. $6\overline{)84}$ $9\overline{)99}$ $3\overline{)45}$ $4\overline{)64}$ $7\overline{)84}$

Practice Page: 2–Digit Division with and without Remainders
Divide.

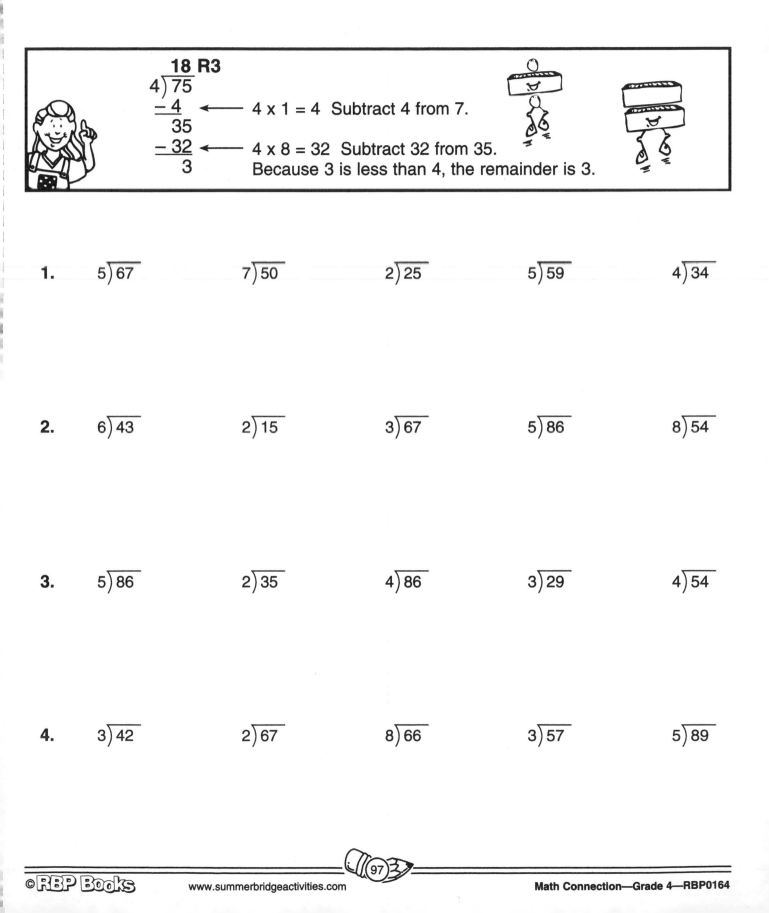

$$\begin{array}{r} 18\ \textbf{R3} \\ 4\overline{)75} \\ -4 \\ \hline 35 \\ -32 \\ \hline 3 \end{array}$$

4 x 1 = 4 Subtract 4 from 7.

4 x 8 = 32 Subtract 32 from 35.
Because 3 is less than 4, the remainder is 3.

1. $5\overline{)67}$ $7\overline{)50}$ $2\overline{)25}$ $5\overline{)59}$ $4\overline{)34}$

2. $6\overline{)43}$ $2\overline{)15}$ $3\overline{)67}$ $5\overline{)86}$ $8\overline{)54}$

3. $5\overline{)86}$ $2\overline{)35}$ $4\overline{)86}$ $3\overline{)29}$ $4\overline{)54}$

4. $3\overline{)42}$ $2\overline{)67}$ $8\overline{)66}$ $3\overline{)57}$ $5\overline{)89}$

Practice Page: 2–Digit Division with and without Remainders

Divide.

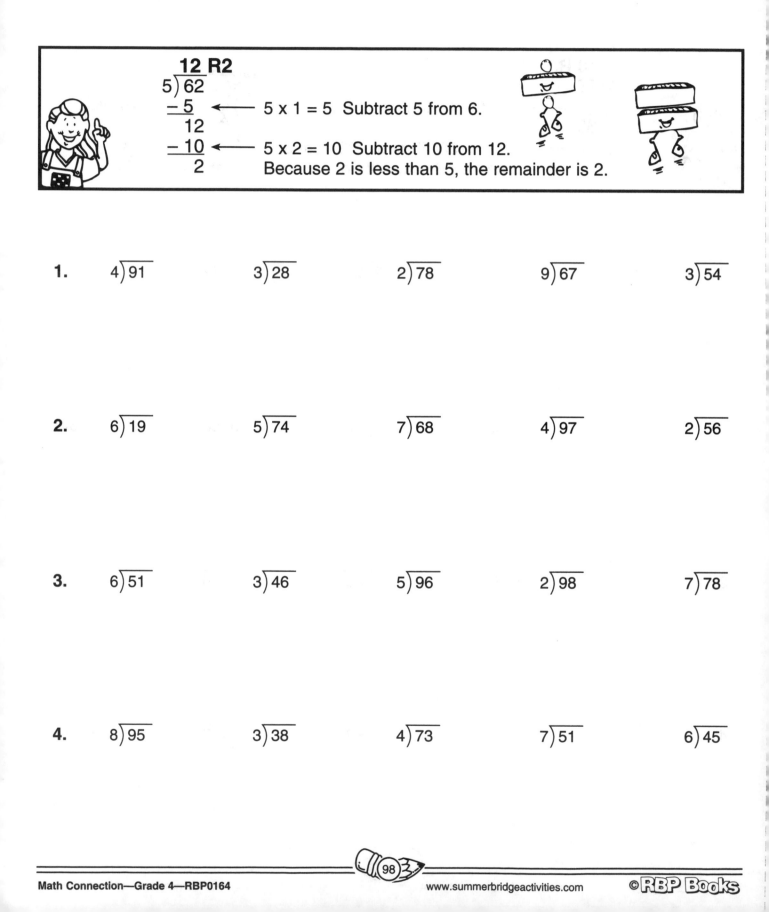

```
    12 R2
5) 62
  − 5    ←—— 5 x 1 = 5  Subtract 5 from 6.
   12
  − 10   ←—— 5 x 2 = 10  Subtract 10 from 12.
    2            Because 2 is less than 5, the remainder is 2.
```

1. 4) 91   3) 28   2) 78   9) 67   3) 54

2. 6) 19   5) 74   7) 68   4) 97   2) 56

3. 6) 51   3) 46   5) 96   2) 98   7) 78

4. 8) 95   3) 38   4) 73   7) 51   6) 45

Math Connection—Grade 4—RBP0164   www.summerbridgeactivities.com   ©RBP Books

Name _____   Date _____

Practice Page: 3–Digit Division without Remainders
Divide.

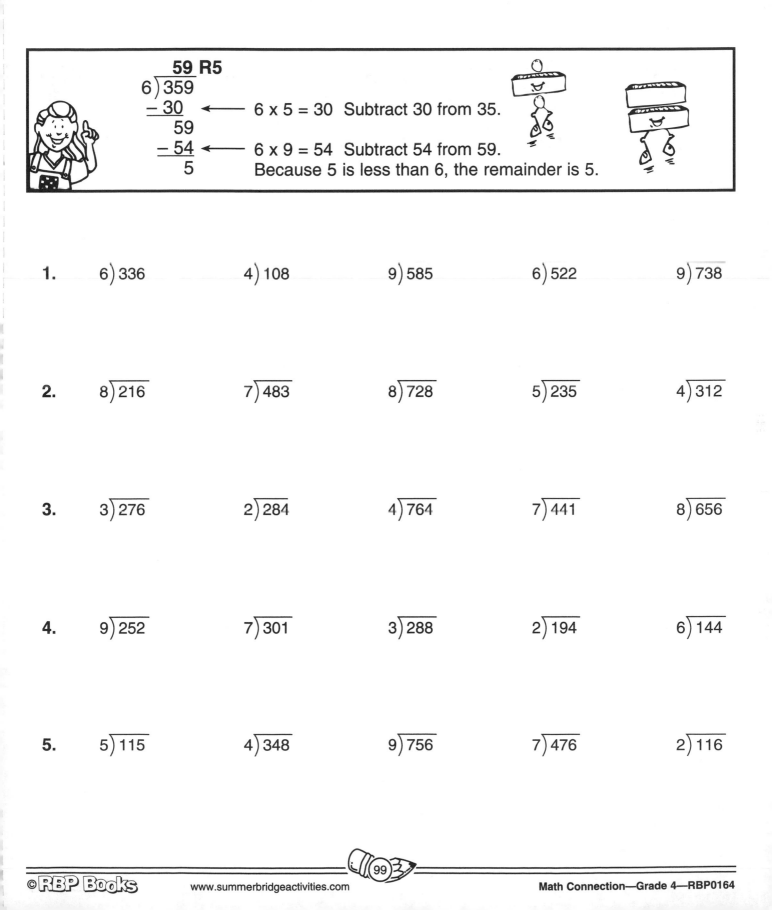

$$\begin{array}{r} \mathbf{59\ R5} \\ 6\overline{)359} \\ -30 \\ \hline 59 \\ -54 \\ \hline 5 \end{array}$$

6 x 5 = 30   Subtract 30 from 35.

6 x 9 = 54   Subtract 54 from 59.
Because 5 is less than 6, the remainder is 5.

1. $6\overline{)336}$ $4\overline{)108}$ $9\overline{)585}$ $6\overline{)522}$ $9\overline{)738}$

2. $8\overline{)216}$ $7\overline{)483}$ $8\overline{)728}$ $5\overline{)235}$ $4\overline{)312}$

3. $3\overline{)276}$ $2\overline{)284}$ $4\overline{)764}$ $7\overline{)441}$ $8\overline{)656}$

4. $9\overline{)252}$ $7\overline{)301}$ $3\overline{)288}$ $2\overline{)194}$ $6\overline{)144}$

5. $5\overline{)115}$ $4\overline{)348}$ $9\overline{)756}$ $7\overline{)476}$ $2\overline{)116}$

Practice Page: 3–Digit Division with and without Remainders
Divide.

1. $2\overline{)654}$ $5\overline{)671}$ $3\overline{)964}$ $8\overline{)937}$ $4\overline{)617}$

2. $4\overline{)672}$ $7\overline{)743}$ $9\overline{)367}$ $3\overline{)421}$ $6\overline{)876}$

3. $8\overline{)864}$ $6\overline{)917}$ $2\overline{)415}$ $5\overline{)981}$ $4\overline{)633}$

4. $2\overline{)505}$ $9\overline{)121}$ $3\overline{)226}$ $9\overline{)215}$ $5\overline{)809}$

5. $8\overline{)647}$ $5\overline{)537}$ $3\overline{)601}$ $7\overline{)632}$ $4\overline{)498}$

Math Connection—Grade 4—RBP0164   www.summerbridgeactivities.com   © RBP Books

Practice Page: 3–Digit Division with and without Remainders

Divide.

1. $2\overline{)985}$ $4\overline{)249}$ $8\overline{)127}$ $6\overline{)214}$ $6\overline{)795}$

2. $3\overline{)384}$ $6\overline{)822}$ $8\overline{)110}$ $4\overline{)947}$ $9\overline{)114}$

3. $7\overline{)631}$ $2\overline{)133}$ $4\overline{)506}$ $8\overline{)243}$ $5\overline{)204}$

4. $4\overline{)977}$ $9\overline{)267}$ $2\overline{)952}$ $6\overline{)614}$ $3\overline{)674}$

5. $5\overline{)593}$ $3\overline{)866}$ $7\overline{)404}$ $3\overline{)917}$ $7\overline{)788}$

www.summerbridgeactivities.com   Math Connection—Grade 4—RBP0164

Practice Page: 2– and 3–Digit Division with and without Remainders

Divide.

1. $4\overline{)76}$ $3\overline{)91}$ $5\overline{)86}$ $6\overline{)50}$ $2\overline{)35}$

2. $7\overline{)85}$ $2\overline{)49}$ $4\overline{)34}$ $8\overline{)43}$ $5\overline{)79}$

3. $4\overline{)312}$ $8\overline{)674}$ $3\overline{)497}$ $4\overline{)406}$ $2\overline{)677}$

4. $6\overline{)557}$ $3\overline{)325}$ $5\overline{)235}$ $2\overline{)407}$ $8\overline{)216}$

5. $3\overline{)276}$ $8\overline{)728}$ $4\overline{)108}$ $7\overline{)441}$ $5\overline{)336}$

Math Connection—Grade 4—RBP0164   www.summerbridgeactivities.com   ©RBP Books

Problem Solving: 2– and 3–Digit Division with and without Remainders

Solve each problem.

1. There are 45 reptiles at the zoo. Altogether there are the same number of lizards, snakes, and chameleons. How many snakes are there at the zoo?

2. The Smithfield Zoo buys 7 times as much birdseed as the Parker Zoo. If the Smithfield Zoo buys 553 pounds of birdseed, how many pounds of birdseed does the Parker Zoo buy?

3. Andy feeds the penguins 249 pounds of food during 3 months. If he feeds the penguins the same amount of food each month, how many pounds of food does he feed them each month?

4. In January, 233 people visited the zoo. 148 people came in February, and 249 people came in March. What was the average number of people that visited the zoo each month? (Hint: Add, then divide the total by 3.)

5. Lexie sold 39 plastic animals in the souvenir shop. If each customer bought 3 animals, how many customers came into the gift shop?

6. Marina has 140 pounds of meat. If she divides the meat between 9 cages, how many pounds of meat can she put in each cage? How much meat will be left?

7. Mark sold 145 red balloons, 348 yellow balloons, and 287 blue balloons. If each person bought 3 balloons, how many people bought balloons?

8. The zoo orders 567 pounds of fish. If the zookeeper divides the fish into 9 buckets, how many pounds of fish are in each bucket?

www.summerbridgeactivities.com   Math Connection—Grade 4—RBP0164

Problem Solving: 2– and 3–Digit Division with and without Remainders

Solve each problem.

1.

Katie boxed 273 umbrellas. If she put 7 umbrellas in each box, how many boxes of umbrellas did she have when she finished?

2.

It snowed 96 inches at the ski resort. How many feet did it snow?

3.

Jordan recorded the temperatures for 5 days: 94, 88, 90, 97, and 86 degrees F. What was the average daily temperature? (Hint: Add, then divide the total by 5.)

4.

It was 2 times as hot in the desert as in the mountains. If it was 110 degrees F in the desert, how hot was it in the mountains?

5.

There was 188 feet of sidewalk to shovel after the snowstorm. If 4 people help shovel the sidewalk, how many feet will each person have to shovel?

6.

Jordan recorded the same amount of rainfall each month for the last 7 months. If the total amount of rainfall was 91 inches, how many inches did it rain in 1 month?

7.

In March, it rained 15 inches. It rained 12 inches in April and 18 inches in May. What was the average monthly rainfall? (Hint: Add, then divide the total by 3.)

8.

Max boxed 594 snow shovels. If he put 8 snow shovels in each box, how many boxes of snow shovels did he have when he finished? How many shovels did he have left over?

Name _____   Date _____

Post-Test: 2– and 3–Digit Division with and without Remainders
Divide.

1. $2\overline{)45}$ $2\overline{)64}$ $7\overline{)85}$ $8\overline{)14}$ $4\overline{)70}$

2. $7\overline{)67}$ $6\overline{)85}$ $3\overline{)28}$ $9\overline{)75}$ $2\overline{)59}$

3. $9\overline{)585}$ $7\overline{)483}$ $9\overline{)738}$ $8\overline{)656}$ $6\overline{)522}$

4. $4\overline{)396}$ $2\overline{)178}$ $5\overline{)140}$ $4\overline{)268}$ $7\overline{)182}$

5. $8\overline{)837}$ $2\overline{)551}$ $6\overline{)495}$ $9\overline{)100}$ $5\overline{)612}$

Measurement: Metric Measures

> 1 gram (g) = 1,000 milligrams (mg)
>
> 1,000 grams (g) = 1 kilogram (kg)

Find the missing numbers.

1. 3 g = _____ mg   8,000 mg = _____ g   14,000 g = _____ kg

2. 84,000 g = _____ kg   9 g = _____ mg   41,000 g = _____ kg

3. 73 g = _____ mg   57,000 mg = _____ g   25,000 g = _____ kg

4. 7,000 g = _____ kg   12 g = _____ mg   118,000 g = _____ kg

5. 6,000 g = _____ kg   2,000 mg = _____ g   65 g = _____ mg

Answer each question.

6. Megan uses 4,000 milligrams of sugar in her recipe. How many grams of sugar does she use?

7. Harry measures 15 grams of salt. How many milligrams does he measure?

8. Jake's book weighs 2 kilograms. How many grams does his book weigh?

9. Peter's recipe calls for 16,000 milligrams of cocoa. How many grams of cocoa does Peter need?

Measurement: Metric Measures

10 millimeters (mm) = 1 centimeter (cm)
100 centimeters (cm) = 1 meter (m)
1,000 meters (m) = 1 kilometer (km)

Find the missing numbers.

1. 5 cm = _____ mm   700 cm = _____ m   8,000 m = _____ km

2. 16,000 m = _____ km   60 mm = _____ cm   36 cm = _____ mm

3. 400 cm = _____ m   2 km = _____ m   15 m = _____ cm

4. 90 mm = _____ cm   72 m = _____ cm   4 km = _____ m

5. 9 m = _____ cm   5,000 m = _____ km   84 cm = _____ mm

6. 17 km = _____ m   3 cm = _____ mm   61 m = _____ cm

Answer each question.

7.
Penny walks 2 kilometers. Angela walks 5,000 meters. How many more meters does Angela walk than Penny? How many meters do they walk altogether?

8.
Norman's piece of string measures 15 centimeters. Kayla's piece of string is 200 millimeters. Who has the longest piece of string?

Measurement: Metric Measures

1 liter (L) = 1,000 milliliters (mL)

Find the missing numbers.

1. 8 L = _____ mL   5,000 mL = _____ L   15 L = _____ mL

2. 48,000 mL = _____ L   4 L = _____ mL   33,000 mL = _____ L

3. 92 L = _____ mL   21 L = _____ mL   7,000 mL = _____ L

4. 6 L = _____ mL   8,000 mL = _____ L   27 L = _____ mL

Answer each question.

5.
William measures 18,000 milliliters of milk. How many liters does he measure?

6.
Karen drinks $\frac{1}{2}$ of a liter of soda. How many milliliters does she drink?

7.
Mark pours 14 liters of juice at the party. How many milliliters of juice does he pour?

8.
Isabelle buys 15 2-liter bottles of soda for the party. Her guests drink 18,000 milliliters. How many liters of soda does Isabelle have left over? How many 2-liter bottles does she have left over?

Pre-Test: 3– and 4–Digit Division with and without Remainders

Divide.

1. $3\overline{)309}$ $5\overline{)155}$ $2\overline{)518}$ $8\overline{)168}$ $4\overline{)364}$

2. $3\overline{)1,236}$ $9\overline{)1,387}$ $3\overline{)3,642}$ $7\overline{)1,348}$ $2\overline{)2,248}$

3. $5\overline{)1,625}$ $4\overline{)6,871}$ $8\overline{)9,471}$ $3\overline{)2,898}$ $5\overline{)4,064}$

4. $3\overline{)9,471}$ $8\overline{)5,096}$ $7\overline{)1,547}$ $4\overline{)6,078}$ $9\overline{)9,715}$

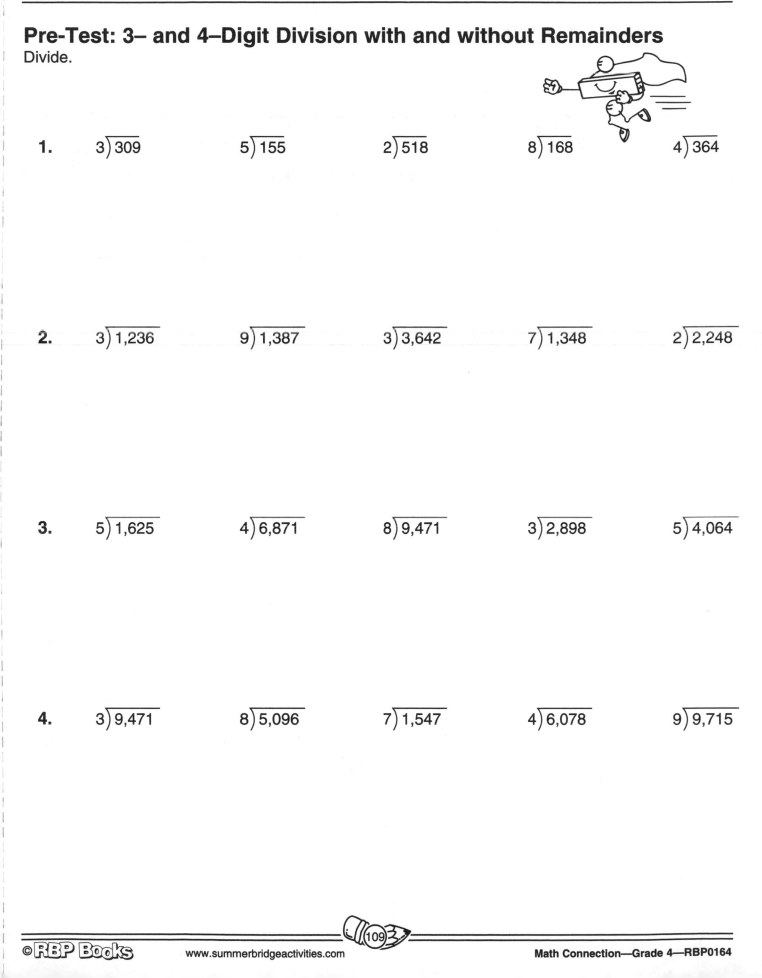

www.summerbridgeactivities.com **Math Connection—Grade 4—RBP0164**

Name _____   Date _____

Practice Page: 3–Digit Division without Remainders
Divide.

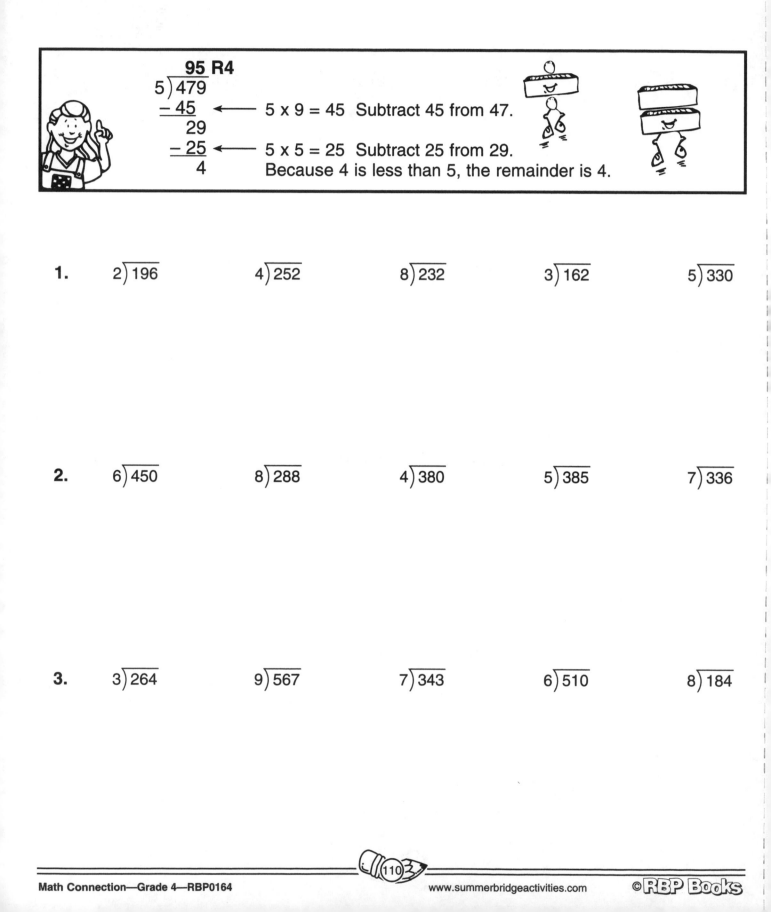

```
    95 R4
5)479
  - 45    ◄─── 5 x 9 = 45   Subtract 45 from 47.
    29
  - 25    ◄─── 5 x 5 = 25   Subtract 25 from 29.
     4         Because 4 is less than 5, the remainder is 4.
```

1. 2)196   4)252   8)232   3)162   5)330

2. 6)450   8)288   4)380   5)385   7)336

3. 3)264   9)567   7)343   6)510   8)184

Name _____   Date _____

Practice Page: 3–Digit Division with and without Remainders
Divide.

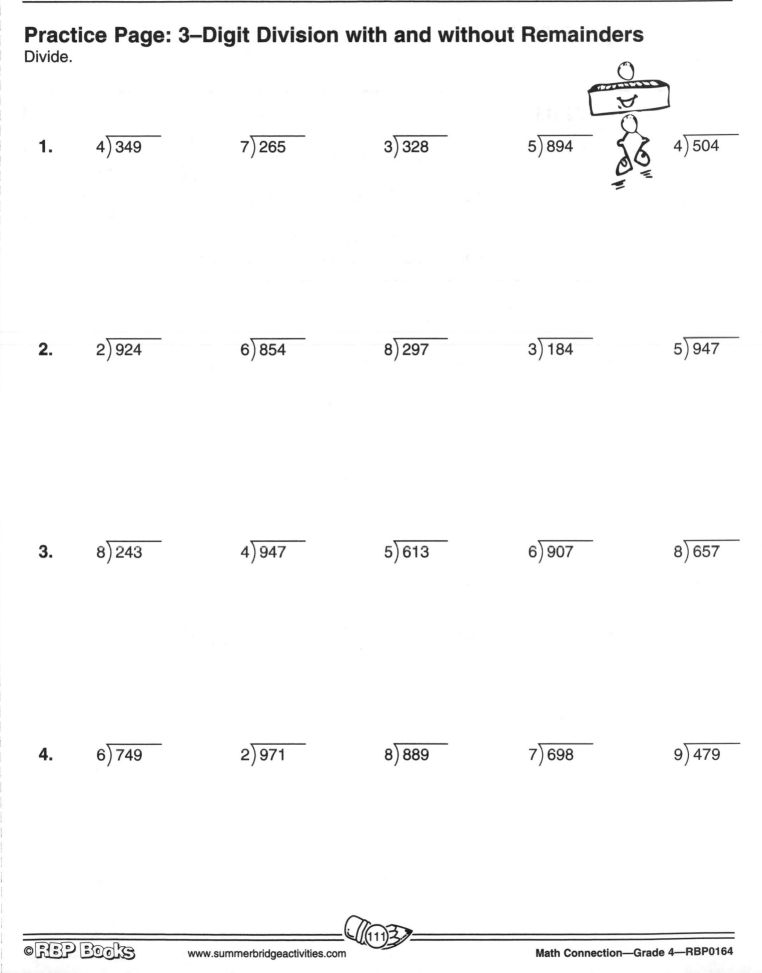

1.   4)349   7)265   3)328   5)894   4)504

2.   2)924   6)854   8)297   3)184   5)947

3.   8)243   4)947   5)613   6)907   8)657

4.   6)749   2)971   8)889   7)698   9)479

Practice Page: 4–Digit Division with and without Remainders

Divide.

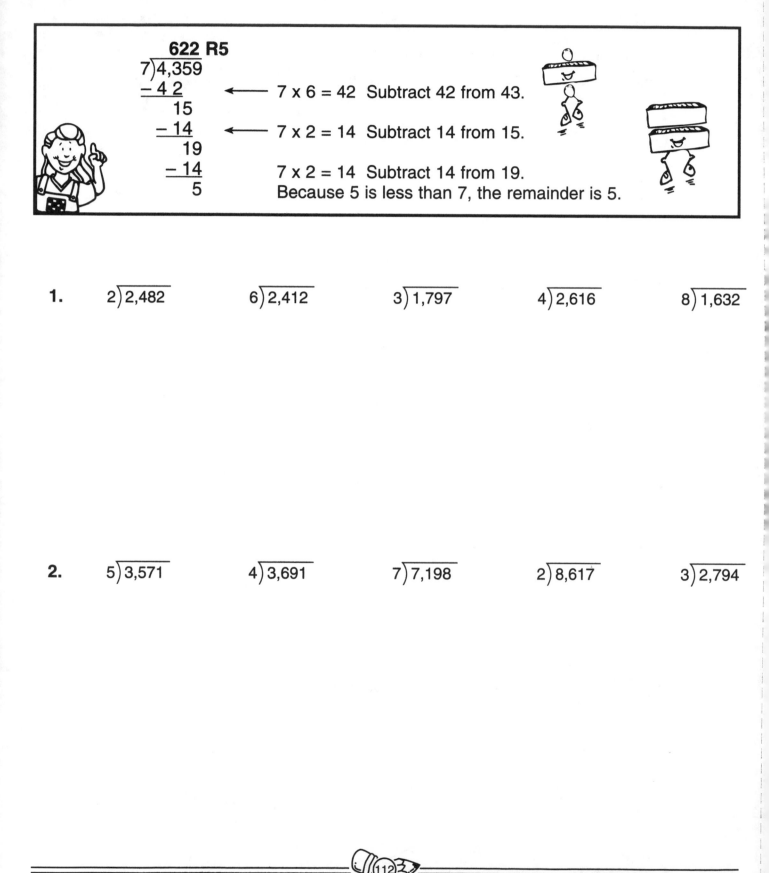

622 R5

$7\overline{)4,359}$
$\underline{-42}$ ← 7 x 6 = 42 Subtract 42 from 43.
15
$\underline{-14}$ ← 7 x 2 = 14 Subtract 14 from 15.
19
$\underline{-14}$ 7 x 2 = 14 Subtract 14 from 19.
5   Because 5 is less than 7, the remainder is 5.

1. $2\overline{)2,482}$ $6\overline{)2,412}$ $3\overline{)1,797}$ $4\overline{)2,616}$ $8\overline{)1,632}$

2. $5\overline{)3,571}$ $4\overline{)3,691}$ $7\overline{)7,198}$ $2\overline{)8,617}$ $3\overline{)2,794}$

Math Connection—Grade 4—RBP0164   www.summerbridgeactivities.com   ©RBP Books

Practice Page: 3– and 4–Digit Division with and without Remainders

Divide.

1. $3\overline{)264}$ $8\overline{)576}$ $2\overline{)178}$ $7\overline{)301}$ $6\overline{)528}$

2. $4\overline{)396}$ $8\overline{)176}$ $9\overline{)225}$ $3\overline{)222}$ $2\overline{)402}$

3. $7\overline{)721}$ $6\overline{)330}$ $8\overline{)432}$ $5\overline{)190}$ $4\overline{)848}$

4. $3\overline{)9,273}$ $4\overline{)1,684}$ $2\overline{)1,248}$ $5\overline{)1,805}$ $6\overline{)1,458}$

5. $8\overline{)1,806}$ $5\overline{)5,971}$ $6\overline{)9,781}$ $3\overline{)1,688}$ $4\overline{)8,437}$

The digits are really coming down today!

© RBP Books   www.summerbridgeactivities.com   Math Connection—Grade 4—RBP0164

Practice Page: 3– and 4–Digit Division with and without Remainders
Divide.

1. $2\overline{)468}$ $5\overline{)375}$ $8\overline{)179}$ $6\overline{)781}$ $3\overline{)407}$

2. $7\overline{)354}$ $4\overline{)267}$ $3\overline{)141}$ $2\overline{)926}$ $5\overline{)987}$

3. $6\overline{)987}$ $5\overline{)176}$ $9\overline{)167}$ $8\overline{)768}$ $4\overline{)167}$

4. $5\overline{)1,186}$ $3\overline{)4,892}$ $6\overline{)7,981}$ $8\overline{)9,707}$ $4\overline{)3,671}$

Math Connection—Grade 4—RBP0164   www.summerbridgeactivities.com   ©RBP Books

Name _____ Date _____

Practice Page: 3– and 4–Digit Division with and without Remainders
Divide.

1. $3\overline{)267}$ $2\overline{)843}$ $6\overline{)238}$ $4\overline{)779}$ $5\overline{)611}$

2. $4\overline{)267}$ $8\overline{)798}$ $2\overline{)279}$ $7\overline{)507}$ $8\overline{)115}$

3. $9\overline{)915}$ $5\overline{)687}$ $7\overline{)214}$ $3\overline{)542}$ $4\overline{)127}$

4. $2\overline{)6,715}$ $8\overline{)9,417}$ $6\overline{)6,413}$ $4\overline{)1,676}$ $5\overline{)6,878}$

www.summerbridgeactivities.com   **Math Connection—Grade 4—RBP0164**

Practice Page: 4–Digit Division with and without Remainders

Divide.

1. $4\overline{)1{,}682}$ $3\overline{)2{,}412}$ $7\overline{)1{,}492}$ $6\overline{)2{,}416}$ $5\overline{)3{,}532}$

2. $8\overline{)3{,}579}$ $5\overline{)2{,}541}$ $3\overline{)6{,}507}$ $4\overline{)9{,}817}$ $6\overline{)3{,}689}$

3. $2\overline{)9{,}473}$ $4\overline{)6{,}495}$ $8\overline{)9{,}173}$ $5\overline{)5{,}971}$ $9\overline{)2{,}717}$

4. $7\overline{)2{,}215}$ $3\overline{)4{,}795}$ $5\overline{)5{,}517}$ $8\overline{)1{,}443}$ $4\overline{)6{,}179}$

Practice Page: 3– and 4–Digit Division with and without Remainders
Divide.

1. $3\overline{)654}$ $5\overline{)255}$ $4\overline{)670}$ $8\overline{)917}$ $2\overline{)127}$

2. $6\overline{)2,487}$ $4\overline{)1,674}$ $8\overline{)1,971}$ $7\overline{)5,179}$ $5\overline{)4,075}$

3. $3\overline{)3,955}$ $9\overline{)6,122}$ $7\overline{)9,479}$ $4\overline{)1,236}$ $5\overline{)6,469}$

4. $8\overline{)6,492}$ $5\overline{)1,840}$ $6\overline{)1,294}$ $7\overline{)6,804}$ $3\overline{)9,014}$

Practice Page: 3– and 4–Digit Division with and without Remainders
Divide.

1. $6\overline{)497}$ $2\overline{)128}$ $5\overline{)257}$ $9\overline{)418}$ $6\overline{)678}$

2. $5\overline{)2,516}$ $3\overline{)8,437}$ $3\overline{)2,076}$ $8\overline{)8,179}$ $6\overline{)2,649}$

3. $9\overline{)5,082}$ $7\overline{)6,554}$ $5\overline{)9,479}$ $2\overline{)4,236}$ $3\overline{)6,879}$

4. $2\overline{)6,671}$ $4\overline{)3,424}$ $8\overline{)3,456}$ $5\overline{)9,466}$ $9\overline{)3,952}$

Math Connection—Grade 4—RBP0164   www.summerbridgeactivities.com

Problem Solving: 3– and 4–Digit Division with and without Remainders

Solve each problem.

1.

Kyle is packaging jam in cartons. If each carton holds 9 bottles of jam, how many cartons will he need to package 1,934 bottles of jam?

2.

Anna has 7,209 cans of soup that need to be boxed. If she puts 9 cans of soup in 1 box, how many boxes will she need?

3.

Katherine has 9,315 sunflower seeds. She puts 7 seeds in each package. How many full packages of sunflower seeds does Katherine have when she's finished? How many seeds are left over?

4.

Jackson is bottling 6,488 ounces of root beer. One bottle holds 8 ounces. How many bottles will Jackson have if he bottles all of the root beer?

5.

Mario is packaging footballs in a box. Six footballs will fit in one box. How many boxes will Mario need if he has to package 288 footballs?

6.

Katie has 2,837 flowers. If Katie puts 7 flowers in each vase, how many full vases will Katie have when she's finished? How many flowers will be left?

7.

Linus is bottling soda. Each bottle holds 7 ounces. How many bottles does Linus need if he has 2,786 ounces of soda to bottle?

8.

Jenny is packaging fruit. She has 349 apples, 328 pears, and 548 oranges. If she puts 4 pieces of fruit in each package, how many full packages will she have when she's finished? How many pieces of fruit will be left?

Problem Solving: 3– and 4–Digit Division with and without Remainders

Solve each problem.

1.

Marty and his family drove 2,544 miles in 4 days. If they drove the same number of miles each day, how many miles did they drive each day?

2.

Dayna took 288 pictures on her 4-day vacation. She took the same number of pictures each day. How many pictures did Dayna take each day?

3.

Carrie sold 1,960 postcards to tourists. Each tourist bought 5 postcards. How many tourists bought postcards?

4.

There were 474 passengers on the airplane. If there were 6 people on each row, how many rows were there on the airplane?

5.

Chris drove the same number of miles each hour. If he drove for 8 hours and traveled 528 miles altogether, how many miles did he drive in each hour?

6.

The cruise ship had 3,392 pieces of luggage. If each passenger brought aboard 2 pieces of luggage each, how many passengers were there on the cruise ship?

7.

Rachael sold 546 souvenirs in the gift shop. Each customer bought 6 souvenirs. How many customers came to the gift shop?

8.

Sarah traveled 1,241 miles on Tuesday, 848 miles on Wednesday, and 761 miles on Thursday. What was the average number of miles she traveled per day? (Hint: Add, then divide the total by the number of days.)

Post-Test: 3– and 4–Digit Division with and without Remainders

Divide.

1. $4\overline{)514}$ $3\overline{)267}$ $5\overline{)305}$ $7\overline{)947}$ $2\overline{)678}$

2. $3\overline{)2,716}$ $5\overline{)9,178}$ $6\overline{)3,644}$ $9\overline{)5,415}$ $7\overline{)5,106}$

3. $2\overline{)1,484}$ $4\overline{)6,457}$ $7\overline{)9,402}$ $5\overline{)4,935}$ $3\overline{)1,057}$

4. $6\overline{)2,123}$ $8\overline{)9,734}$ $2\overline{)1,485}$ $6\overline{)3,312}$ $4\overline{)3,648}$

Multiplication and Division

Divide. Then, multiply to check your answer.

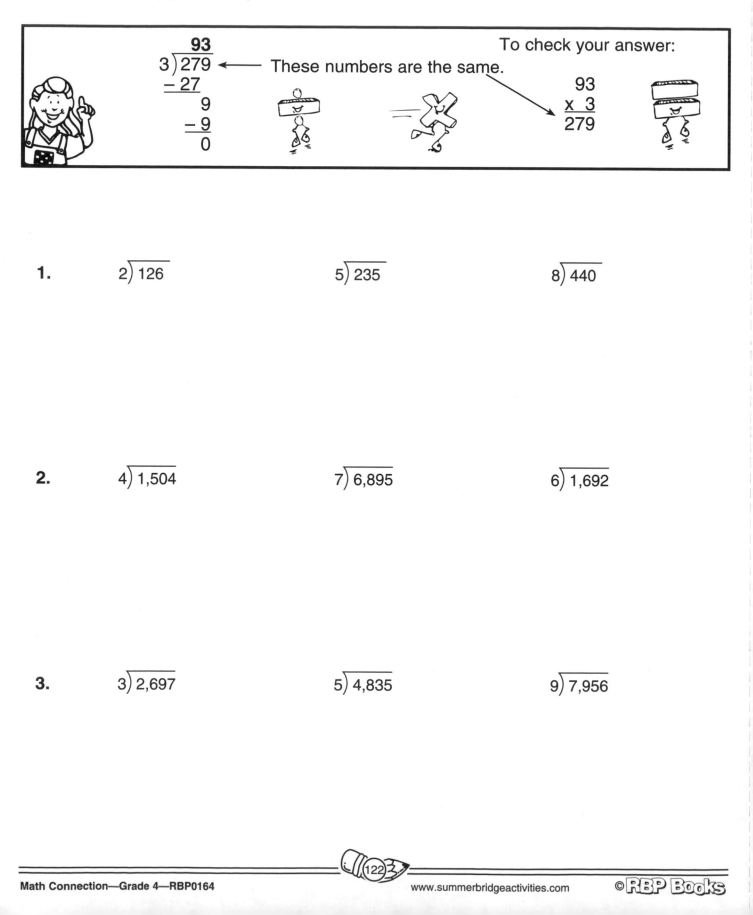

$$\begin{array}{r} 93 \\ 3\overline{)279} \\ -27 \\ \hline 9 \\ -9 \\ \hline 0 \end{array}$$

← These numbers are the same.

To check your answer:

$$\begin{array}{r} 93 \\ \times\ 3 \\ \hline 279 \end{array}$$

1. $2\overline{)126}$ $5\overline{)235}$ $8\overline{)440}$

2. $4\overline{)1,504}$ $7\overline{)6,895}$ $6\overline{)1,692}$

3. $3\overline{)2,697}$ $5\overline{)4,835}$ $9\overline{)7,956}$

Multiplication and Division

Divide. Then, multiply to check your answer.

47 R1

$4\overline{)189}$ ← These numbers
$\underline{-16}$ are the same.
  29
$\underline{-28}$
   1

To check your answer:
  47
$\underline{\times\ 4}$
 188
$\underline{+\ 1}$ ← Add your remainder here.
 189

1. $4\overline{)419}$ $3\overline{)956}$ $2\overline{)167}$

2. $5\overline{)6,487}$ $9\overline{)5,075}$ $7\overline{)5,521}$

3. $8\overline{)7,911}$ $4\overline{)1,675}$ $3\overline{)5,539}$

Multiplication and Division

Divide. Then, multiply to check your answer.

1. $2\overline{)214}$ $5\overline{)457}$ $4\overline{)618}$

2. $6\overline{)528}$ $8\overline{)725}$ $3\overline{)499}$

3. $7\overline{)9,448}$ $2\overline{)2,148}$ $5\overline{)3,220}$

4. $6\overline{)5,489}$ $3\overline{)1,966}$ $7\overline{)6,308}$

Name _____ Date _____

Measurement: Finding Perimeter

Find the perimeter of each shape below.

> The **perimeter** is the **distance** around a figure. To find the perimeter of a figure, add up the lengths of all the sides of the figure.
>
> 9 in.
> 3 in.
> 9 + 9 + 3 + 3 = **24 in.**

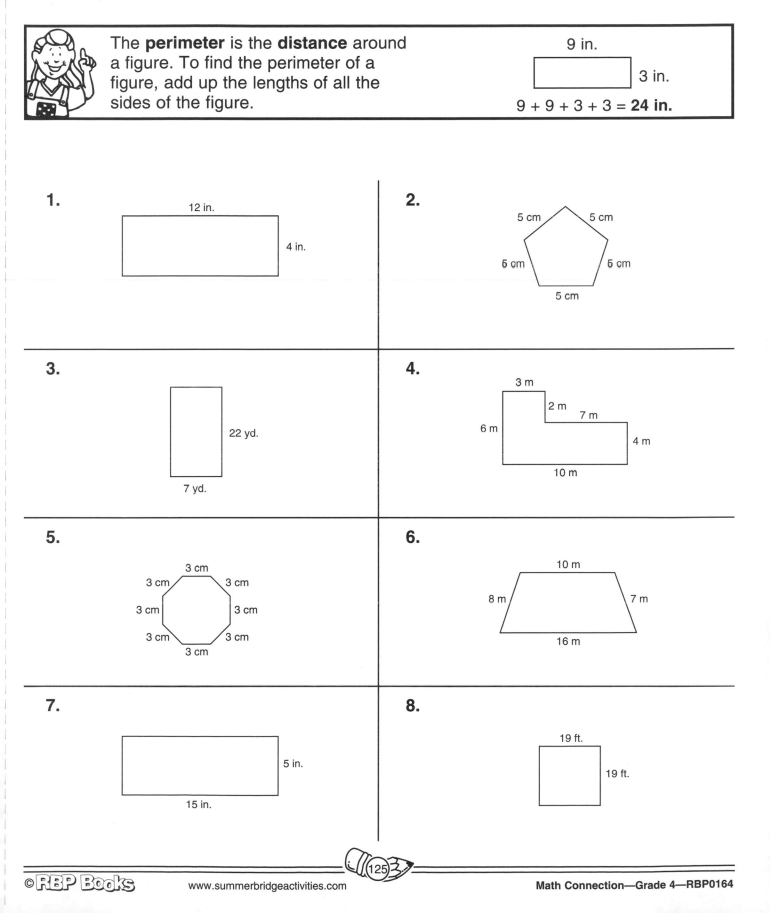

1. 12 in. / 4 in.

2. 5 cm, 5 cm, 5 cm, 5 cm, 5 cm

3. 22 yd. / 7 yd.

4. 3 m, 2 m, 7 m, 6 m, 4 m, 10 m

5. 3 cm, 3 cm, 3 cm, 3 cm, 3 cm, 3 cm, 3 cm, 3 cm

6. 10 m, 8 m, 7 m, 16 m

7. 5 in., 15 in.

8. 19 ft., 19 ft.

Measurement: Finding Perimeter

Remember, to find the **perimeter** of a figure, **add** the lengths of all the sides of the figure.

Find the perimeter.

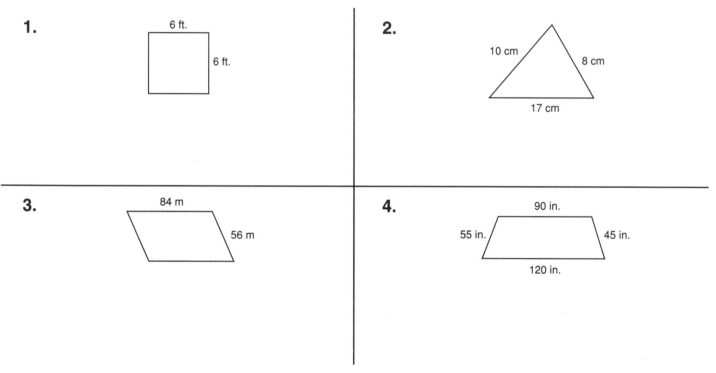

1.   6 ft.
         6 ft.

2.   10 cm   8 cm
         17 cm

3.   84 m
         56 m

4.   90 in.
         55 in.   45 in.
         120 in.

Solve each problem.

5. Jeff is making a rectangular picture frame. If the frame is 36 inches by 24 inches, what is perimeter of the frame?

6. Lisa needs enough trim to go around the edge of her quilt. If the quilt measures 96 inches by 72 inches, how many inches of trim will Lisa need to buy?

7. Gary is building a dog pen. Two of the sides are 45 feet, and the other two sides are 28 feet. How many feet of fencing will Gary need?

8. Randy is gluing string around the edge of his kite. If the sides measure 12 inches, 16 inches, 14 inches, and 13 inches, how many inches of string does Randy need?

Math Connection—Grade 4—RBP0164   www.summerbridgeactivities.com   © RBP Books

Measurement: Finding Perimeter

Solve each problem. Draw a picture to help you find the answer.

1.

Katie is making a planter box out of boards. If her box measures 645 inches long and 359 inches wide, how many inches of board will she need?

2.

Heather buys a rectangular rug that measures 15 feet by 38 feet. What is the perimeter of her rug?

3.

Brandon is putting tile around the edge of his swimming pool. His swimming pool measures 55 feet by 48 feet. How many feet of tile will Brandon need?

4.

Anita is installing a new countertop in her kitchen. What is the perimeter of the countertop if it measures 144 inches by 55 inches?

5.

Hector is fencing an area in his yard. Two of the edges are 37 feet, and the other two edges are 69 feet. If Hector has 225 feet of fencing, how many extra feet of fencing will Hector have?

6.

Helen is putting a border of wallpaper along the top of her kitchen walls. The lengths of her kitchen walls measure 24 feet, 19 feet, 15 feet, and 32 feet. How many feet of wallpaper will Helen need?

7.

Sam is making a square flower bed in his yard. What is the perimeter of his flower bed if each edge measures 27 meters?

8.

Jessica is finishing her tablecloth and needs enough ribbon to go around the edge. If her square tablecloth measures 72 inches by 72 inches, how many **yards** of trim will Lisa need to buy?

Measurement: Finding Area

Find the area of each shape.

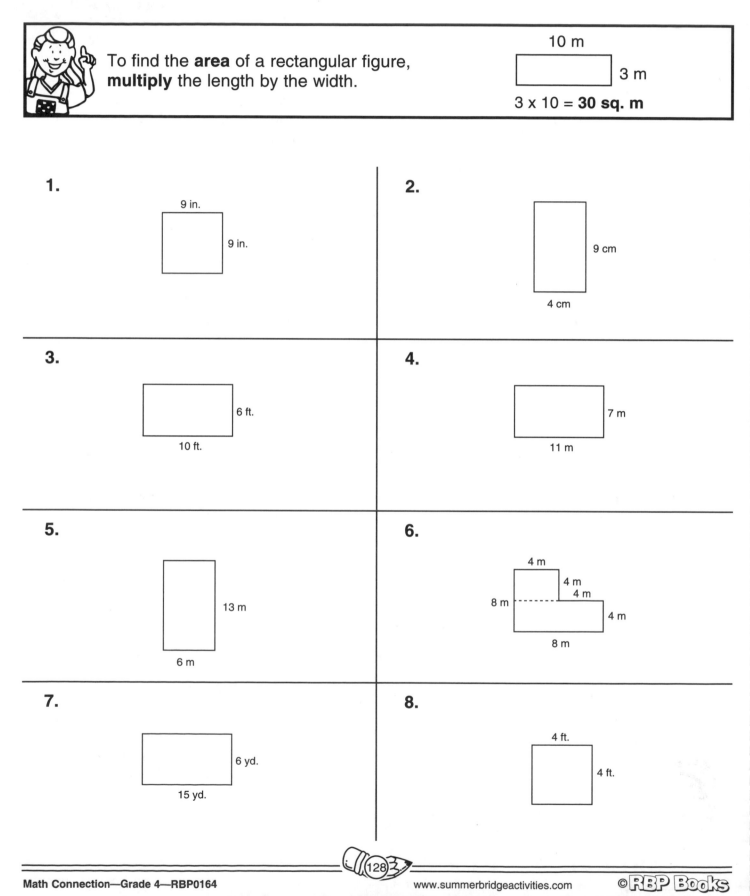

To find the **area** of a rectangular figure, **multiply** the length by the width.

10 m

3 m

3 x 10 = **30 sq. m**

1.

9 in.

9 in.

2.

9 cm

4 cm

3.

6 ft.

10 ft.

4.

7 m

11 m

5.

13 m

6 m

6.

4 m

4 m

4 m

8 m

4 m

8 m

7.

6 yd.

15 yd.

8.

4 ft.

4 ft.

Measurement: Finding Area

Remember, to find the **area** of a rectangular figure, **multiply** the length by the width.

10 m

3 m

3 x 10 = **30 sq. m**

Find the area of each shape.

1.

7 in.

4 in.

2.

8 m

8 m

3.

16 m

5 m

4.

4 cm

4 cm

3 cm

3 cm

Solve each problem.

5.

Helen makes a rectangular kite that is 15 meters by 28 meters. What is the area of Helen's kite?

6.

Lance frames a poster that is 25 inches by 39 inches. What is the area of Lance's poster?

7.

If Maria's garden measures 6 yards by 9 yards, what is the area of her garden?

8.

Travis buys a piece of canvas for his project that measures 15 feet by 33 feet. What is the area of the canvas?

www.summerbridgeactivities.com
Math Connection—Grade 4—RBP0164

Measurement: Finding Perimeter and Area

Solve each problem. Remember to write the unit in your answer.

1.

Jeremy and his friends are building a clubhouse. The finished size is 16 feet by 24 feet. How many square feet will their clubhouse be when it is finished?

2.

Chloe measures an area of the clubhouse for carpet. The area measures 49 inches by 29 inches. How much carpet will Chloe need?

3.

Kevin is painting the clubhouse door blue. The door measures 9 feet by 4 feet. What is the area of the door?

4.

Abby wants to put glass in the window. If her window measures 21 inches by 32 inches, what is the area of the glass she will need?

5.

Marty builds a table that is 27 inches wide and 36 inches long. What is the area of his table?

6.

Pam makes a tablecloth for the new table. Her tablecloth is 42 inches by 33 inches. How many **yards** and **inches** of trim will she need to go around the entire edge of the tablecloth?

7.

Jeremy wants to plant some grass behind the clubhouse. The area is 17 feet by 38 feet. One package of grass seed is enough to plant 200 square feet. How many packages of grass seed will Jeremy need to plant the entire area?

8.

Ryan and Jeremy are going to paint the outside walls of the clubhouse. Two of the walls measure 24 feet by 11 feet. The other two walls measure 16 feet by 11 feet. One gallon of paint will cover 300 square feet. How many gallons of paint will they need?

Math Connection—Grade 4—RBP0164   www.summerbridgeactivities.com   ©RBP Books

Measurement: Standard Capacity

| 12 inches (in.) = 1 foot (ft.) |
| 3 feet (ft.) = 1 yard (yd.) |
| 1,760 yards (yd.) = 1 mile (mi.) |

Find the missing numbers.

1. 24 in. = _____ ft.   6 ft. = _____ in.   8 yd. = _____ ft.

2. 2 yd. = _____ ft.   3 mi. = _____ yd.   45 ft. = _____ yd.

3. 4 ft. = _____ in.   27 ft. = _____ yd.   60 in. = _____ ft.

4. 3,520 yd. = _____ mi.   6 yd. = _____ ft.   5 ft. = _____ in.

5. 7 ft. = _____ in.   30 ft. = _____ yd.   4 mi. = _____ yd.

Answer each question.

6. Peter needs 42 feet of string for his project. How many yards should he buy?

7. Ruby needs 144 inches of ribbon. How many yards does she need to buy?

8. Jamie buys 6 yards of fabric. How many feet of fabric does she have?

9. Juan is 5 feet and 6 inches tall. How many inches tall is Juan?

Measurement: Standard Capacity

1 tablespoon (tbs.) = 3 teaspoons (tsp.)
1 pint (pt.) = 2 cups (c.)
1 quart (qt.) = 2 pints (pt.)
1 gallon (gal.) = 4 quarts (qt.)

Find the missing numbers.

1. 2 tbs. = _____ tsp.   12 c. = _____ pt.   27 tsp. = _____ tbs.

2. 2 pt. = _____ c.   5 tbs. = _____ tsp.   8 qt. = _____ pt.

3. 9 tbs. = _____ tsp.   14 pt. = _____ qt.   7 pt. = _____ c.

4. 10 qt. = _____ pt.   8 qt. = _____ gal.   12 pt. = _____ qt.

5. 14 pt. = _____ c.   3 tbs. = _____ tsp.   24 c. = _____ pt.

Answer each question.

6. If Lindsay has 2 gallons of milk, how many pints does she have?

7. Robin is making cookies for her friends. If her recipe calls for 18 teaspoons of sugar, how many tablespoons should she use?

8. Jeff is making orange juice. If he has 8 quarts, how many 1-cup servings can he pour?

9. Diana is making jam. If her recipe calls for 4 cups of sugar, and she doubles it, how many quarts of sugar will she use?

Measurement: Standard Capacity

| 1 tablespoon (tbs.) = 3 teaspoons (tsp.) |
| 1 pint (pt.) = 2 cups (c.) |
| 1 quart (qt.) = 2 pints (pt.) |
| 1 gallon (gal.) = 4 quarts (qt.) |

Find the missing numbers.

1. 32 qt. = _____ gal.   5 pt. = _____ c.   16 gal. = _____ qt.

2. 7 gal. = _____ qt.   4 tbs. = _____ tsp.   34 c. = _____ pt.

3. 32 pt. = _____ c.   16 c. = _____ pt.   12 tbs. = _____ tsp.

4. 10 tbs. = _____ tsp.   15 pt. = _____ c.   11 gal. = _____ qt.

5. 4 c. = _____ pt.   36 tsp. = _____ tbs.   28 qt. = _____ gal.

Answer each question.

6.
Jordan is making lemonade for his party. He uses 7 quarts of water in his recipe. How many pints of water does he need?

7.
Josie's pie recipe calls for 6 pints of chopped fruit. How many cups of chopped fruit does she need if she doubles her recipe?

8.
Sam needs 28 quarts of hot chocolate for the party. How many gallons should he buy?

9.
Marcy bottles 17 gallons of root beer and 12 gallons of punch. She sells her drinks in quart bottles. How many bottles does she need?

Measurement: Time

> 1 year (yr.) = 12 months (mo.)
> 24 hours (hrs.) = 1 day
> 7 days = 1 week
> 60 minutes (min.) = 1 hour

Find the missing numbers.

1. 24 mo. = _____ yrs.   5 weeks = _____ days   9 yrs. = _____ mo.

2. 14 days = _____ weeks   8 hrs. = _____ min.   49 days = _____ weeks

3. 120 min. = _____ hrs.   60 mo. = _____ yrs.   9 weeks = _____ days

4. 5 hrs. = _____ min.   15 yrs. = _____ mo.   40 hrs. = _____ min.

5. 7 yrs. = _____ mo.   6 weeks = _____ days   240 min. = _____ hrs.

Solve each problem.

6. Gary spent 4 weeks biking for his vacation. How many days was he gone on vacation?

7. Angela went on vacation for 28 days. How many weeks was she gone on vacation?

8. Randy's flight was 480 minutes. How many hours did he spend flying?

9. James kept track of the time he spent exercising. He walked on his treadmill for 45 minutes each day. How many hours and minutes did he spend walking after 14 days?

Identifying Fractions
Write the correct fraction.

A fraction tells about equal parts of a whole. The top number, called the **numerator**, tells how many parts are shaded. The bottom number, called the **denominator**, tells how many parts in all.

numerator ⟶ $\dfrac{1}{6}$
denominator ⟶

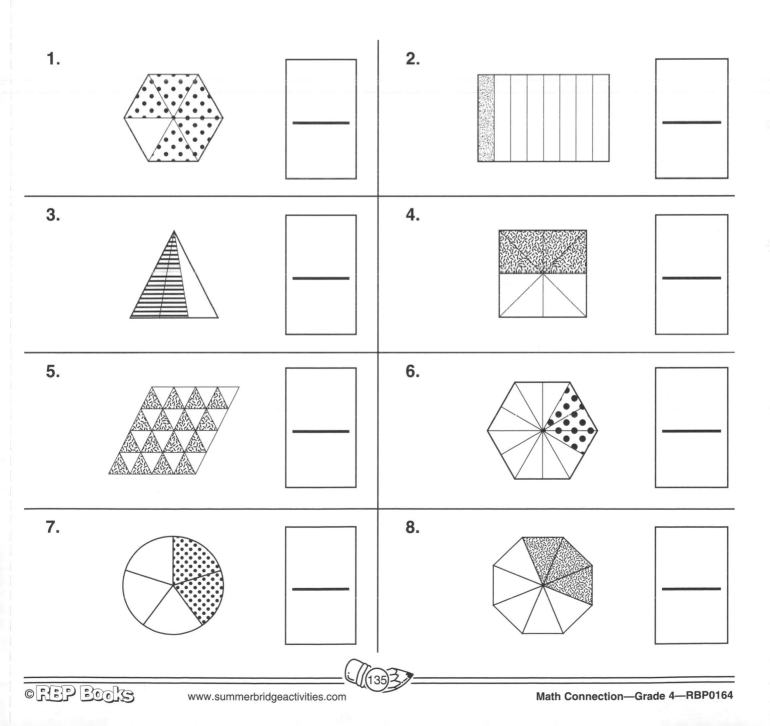

1.

2.

3.

4.

5.

6.

7.

8.

Comparing Fractions

Use the fraction table to help you think about which fraction is greater. Use >, <, or = to compare the fractions.

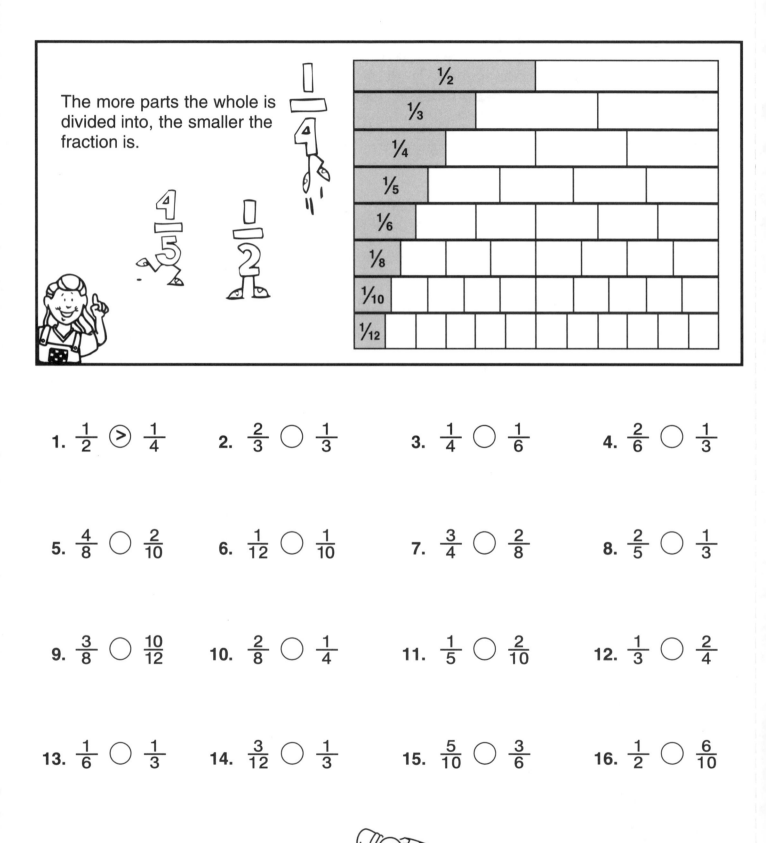

The more parts the whole is divided into, the smaller the fraction is.

1. $\frac{1}{2}$ > $\frac{1}{4}$

2. $\frac{2}{3}$ ◯ $\frac{1}{3}$

3. $\frac{1}{4}$ ◯ $\frac{1}{6}$

4. $\frac{2}{6}$ ◯ $\frac{1}{3}$

5. $\frac{4}{8}$ ◯ $\frac{2}{10}$

6. $\frac{1}{12}$ ◯ $\frac{1}{10}$

7. $\frac{3}{4}$ ◯ $\frac{2}{8}$

8. $\frac{2}{5}$ ◯ $\frac{1}{3}$

9. $\frac{3}{8}$ ◯ $\frac{10}{12}$

10. $\frac{2}{8}$ ◯ $\frac{1}{4}$

11. $\frac{1}{5}$ ◯ $\frac{2}{10}$

12. $\frac{1}{3}$ ◯ $\frac{2}{4}$

13. $\frac{1}{6}$ ◯ $\frac{1}{3}$

14. $\frac{3}{12}$ ◯ $\frac{1}{3}$

15. $\frac{5}{10}$ ◯ $\frac{3}{6}$

16. $\frac{1}{2}$ ◯ $\frac{6}{10}$

www.summerbridgeactivities.com ©RBP Books

Naming Fractions Equal to and Greater than One

Write each fraction as an improper fraction and then as a mixed number.

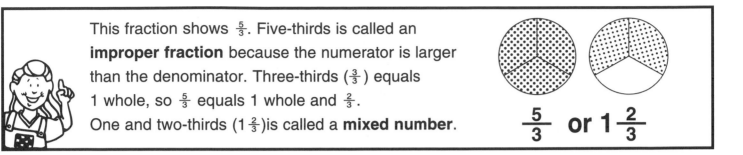

This fraction shows $\frac{5}{3}$. Five-thirds is called an **improper fraction** because the numerator is larger than the denominator. Three-thirds ($\frac{3}{3}$) equals 1 whole, so $\frac{5}{3}$ equals 1 whole and $\frac{2}{3}$. One and two-thirds ($1\frac{2}{3}$) is called a **mixed number**.

$\frac{5}{3}$ or $1\frac{2}{3}$

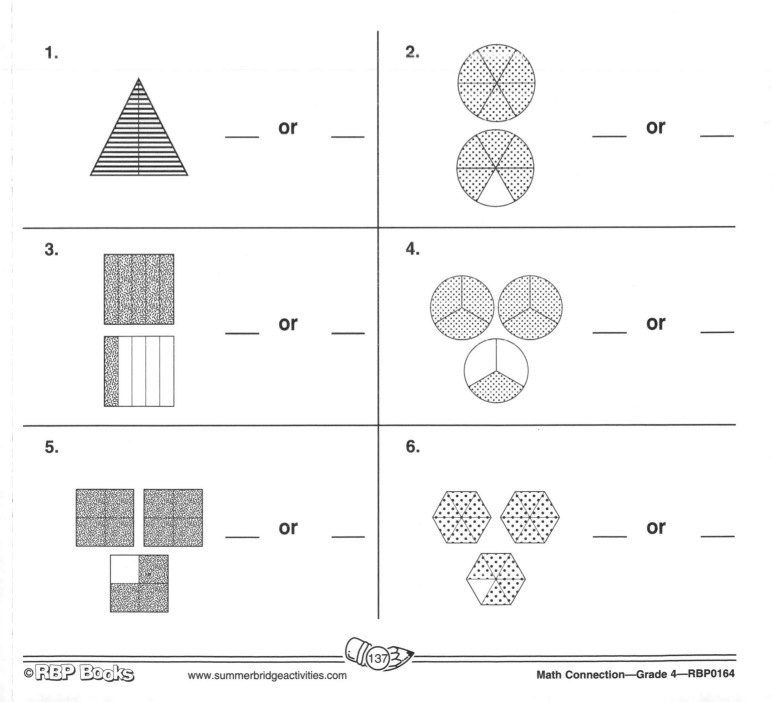

1.   ___ or ___

2.   ___ or ___

3.   ___ or ___

4.   ___ or ___

5.   ___ or ___

6.   ___ or ___

www.summerbridgeactivities.com   **Math Connection—Grade 4—RBP0164**

Rewriting Mixed Numbers

Rewrite each fraction as a mixed number.

To change an improper fraction to a mixed
number, divide the numerator by the denominator,
and place the remainder as the numerator.

14 ÷ 3 = 4 with 2 left over. So $\frac{14}{3}$ can be
renamed $4\frac{2}{3}$.

$$\frac{14}{3} = 4\frac{2}{3}$$

1. $\frac{5}{4}$ =

2. $\frac{10}{3}$ =

3. $\frac{9}{8}$ =

4. $\frac{8}{3}$ =

5. $\frac{5}{2}$ =

6. $\frac{7}{4}$ =

7. $\frac{9}{3}$ =

8. $\frac{11}{10}$ =

9. $\frac{10}{7}$ =

10. $\frac{19}{8}$ =

11. $\frac{9}{5}$ =

12. $\frac{31}{10}$ =

13. $\frac{23}{10}$ =

14. $\frac{17}{8}$ =

15. $\frac{13}{3}$ =

16. $\frac{25}{12}$ =

17. $\frac{28}{9}$ =

18. $\frac{9}{4}$ =

19. $\frac{13}{6}$ =

20. $\frac{76}{25}$ =

Math Connection—Grade 4—RBP0164   www.summerbridgeactivities.com   © RBP Books

Finding Equivalent Fractions

Equivalent fractions are fractions that are equal. To find equivalent fractions, multiply any fraction by 1 or by another name for the number 1. Think about it as multiplying the numerator and the denominator by the same number.

$$\frac{1}{2} \times \frac{2}{2} = \frac{2}{4} \qquad \frac{1}{2} \times \frac{3}{3} = \frac{3}{6} \qquad \frac{1}{2} \times \frac{4}{4} = \frac{4}{8}$$

Cross out the fraction that is not equivalent to the first fraction.

1. $\frac{1}{3} = \frac{2}{6} \quad \frac{3}{9} \quad \frac{4}{8} \quad \frac{5}{15} \quad \frac{6}{18}$

2. $\frac{1}{4} = \frac{2}{8} \quad \frac{3}{6} \quad \frac{4}{16} \quad \frac{5}{20} \quad \frac{6}{24}$

3. $\frac{1}{5} = \frac{2}{6} \quad \frac{2}{10} \quad \frac{3}{15} \quad \frac{4}{20} \quad \frac{5}{25}$

4. $\frac{2}{3} = \frac{4}{6} \quad \frac{6}{9} \quad \frac{8}{16} \quad \frac{10}{15} \quad \frac{12}{18}$

Fill in the missing number.

5. $\frac{1}{4} = \frac{3}{\boxed{}}$

6. $\frac{2}{\boxed{}} = \frac{4}{6}$

7. $\frac{5}{8} = \frac{\boxed{}}{16}$

8. $\frac{3}{4} = \frac{9}{\boxed{}}$

9. $\frac{\boxed{}}{6} = \frac{2}{12}$

10. $\frac{2}{3} = \frac{\boxed{}}{9}$

www.summerbridgeactivities.com

Math Connection—Grade 4—RBP0164

Adding and Subtracting Fractions

Add or subtract. Rewrite improper fractions as mixed numbers.

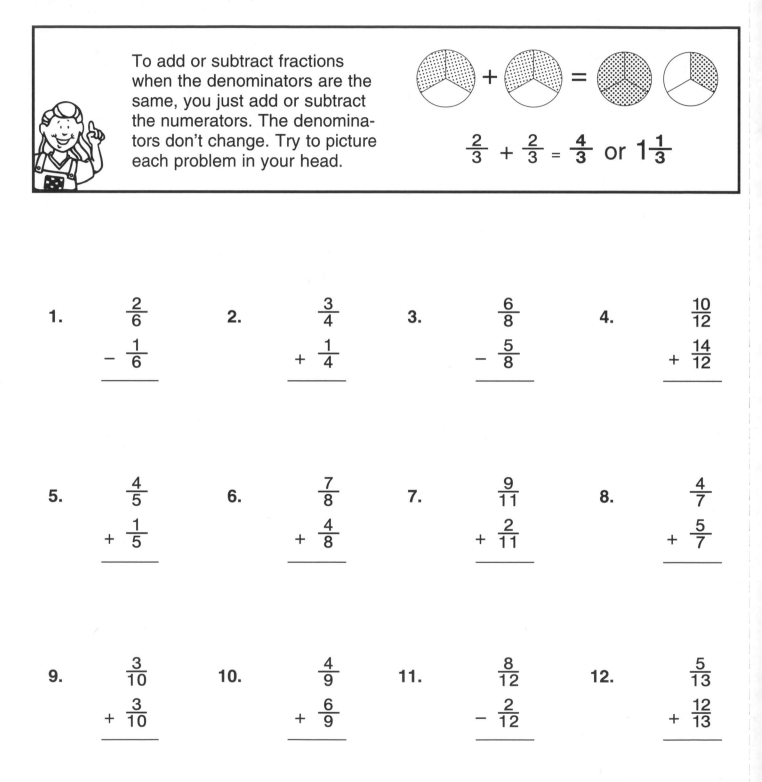

To add or subtract fractions when the denominators are the same, you just add or subtract the numerators. The denominators don't change. Try to picture each problem in your head.

$$\frac{2}{3} + \frac{2}{3} = \frac{4}{3} \text{ or } 1\frac{1}{3}$$

1. $\frac{2}{6}$
   $-\ \frac{1}{6}$

2. $\frac{3}{4}$
   $+\ \frac{1}{4}$

3. $\frac{6}{8}$
   $-\ \frac{5}{8}$

4. $\frac{10}{12}$
   $+\ \frac{14}{12}$

5. $\frac{4}{5}$
   $+\ \frac{1}{5}$

6. $\frac{7}{8}$
   $+\ \frac{4}{8}$

7. $\frac{9}{11}$
   $+\ \frac{2}{11}$

8. $\frac{4}{7}$
   $+\ \frac{5}{7}$

9. $\frac{3}{10}$
   $+\ \frac{3}{10}$

10. $\frac{4}{9}$
   $+\ \frac{6}{9}$

11. $\frac{8}{12}$
   $-\ \frac{2}{12}$

12. $\frac{5}{13}$
   $+\ \frac{12}{13}$

Probability and Statistics

Keshia has 12 pencils in her pencil box. One pencil is red, 3 are blue, 6 are yellow, and 2 are purple.

The probability that she would pull a blue pencil out of the box is $\frac{3}{12}$ because 3 of the 12 pencils are blue.

Probability is the chance or possibility that an event will happen. The probability of something happening can be written as a fraction.

$\frac{3}{12}$ The **numerator** tells the number of chances for a specific event (how many blue pencils).

The **denominator** tells the total number of possible things that could happen (how many total pencils).

- If the fraction that describes the probability is equal to 1, the event is **certain**.
- If the fraction is greater than another, the event is **more likely**.
- If the fraction is less than another, the event is **less likely**.
- If the fraction that describes the probability is 0, the event is **impossible**.

Find the probability.

Penny has 11 pencils in her pencil box. Two pencils are orange, 3 pencils are blue, 5 pencils are yellow, and 1 pencil is green.

1. What is the probability that Penny will pull out an **orange** pencil?

2. What is the probability that Penny will pull out a **green** pencil?

3. What is the probability that Penny will pull out a **blue** pencil?

4. What is the probability that Penny will pull out a **black** pencil?

5. What is the probability that Penny will pull out a **yellow** pencil?

6. What color pencil is Penny **most likely** to pull out of her pencil box?

Probability and Statistics

Use the probabilities from the problems on page 141
to describe whether the event is:

certain   **likely**   **more likely**   **less likely**   **impossible**

1. Pulling a **green** pencil from the box is _____ than pulling a **blue** pencil from the box.

2. Pulling a **yellow** pencil from the box is _____ than pulling a **green** pencil from the box.

3. Pulling a **black** pencil from the box is _____.

4. Pulling an **orange** pencil from the box is _____ than pulling a **blue** pencil from the box.

5. Penny has a new box of 12 pencils, and 12 of the pencils are yellow. Pulling a **yellow** pencil from the box is _____.

Ms. Evan's class took off all of their shoes and put them in a large bag. There were 24 shoes altogether. Ten shoes were sneakers, 2 were dress shoes, 4 were hiking shoes, and 8 were sandals.

6. What is the probability that Nicole will pull a **sneaker** out of the bag?   _____

7. What is the probability that Colton will pull a **dress shoe** out of the bag?   _____

8. What is the probability that Steven will pull a **hiking shoe** out of the bag?   _____

9. What is the probability that Maria will pull a **sandal** out of the bag?   _____

10. What shoe is most likely to be pulled from the bag?   _____

11. What shoe is least likely to be pulled from the bag?   _____

Probability and Statistics

A scientist collected the following data on the length of the whales and dolphins he studied:

blue whale	88 feet
humpback whale	54 feet
gray whale	39 feet
sperm whale	35 feet
beluga whale	13 feet
bottlenose dolphin	9 feet
rough-toothed dolphin	8 feet
Atlantic spotted dolphin	7 feet
spinner dolphin	7 feet

Remember…
- The **range** is the difference between the highest number and the lowest number in the data.
- To calculate the **mean** (or average) add the list of numbers, and then divide by the number of items.
- The **median** is the middle number that appears in the data.
- The **mode** is the number that appears most often in the data

1. What is the range of the data? _____

2. What is the median of the data? _____

3. What is the mode of the data? _____

Use the graph below to answer the questions.

Sam and his friends went whale watching off the coast of Oregon. The bar graph below shows how many gray whales Sam saw.

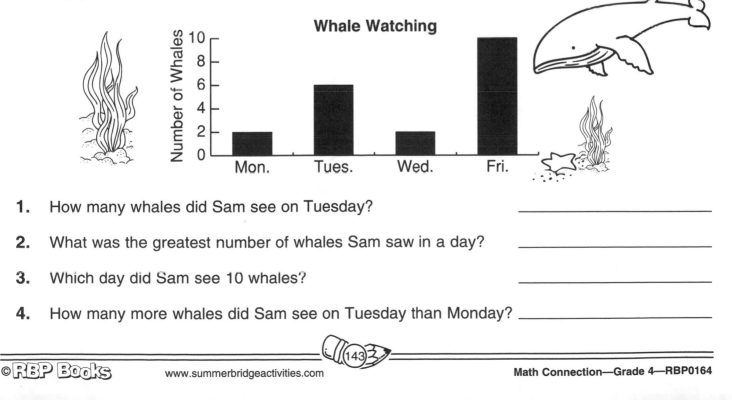

1. How many whales did Sam see on Tuesday? _____

2. What was the greatest number of whales Sam saw in a day? _____

3. Which day did Sam see 10 whales? _____

4. How many more whales did Sam see on Tuesday than Monday? _____

Geometry: Graphing

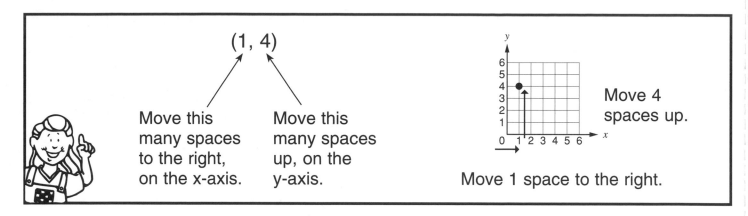

(1, 4)

Move this many spaces to the right, on the x-axis.

Move this many spaces up, on the y-axis.

Move 4 spaces up.

Move 1 space to the right.

Plot the points on the coordinate system below.

1. (4, 0)

2. (3, 2)

3. (5, 5)

4. (0, 4)

5. (2, 1)

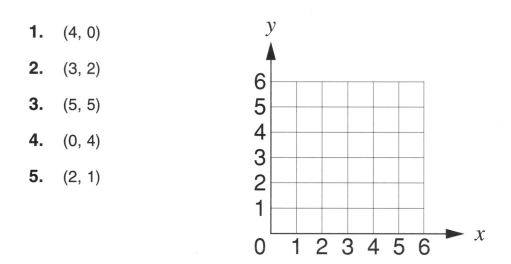

Use the coordinate system below to fill in the missing points.

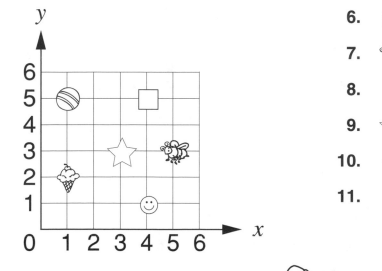

6. ⊘ (_____, _____)

7. 🐝 (_____, _____)

8. ☐ (_____, _____)

9. ☆ (_____, _____)

10. 🍦 (_____, _____)

11. ☺ (_____, _____)

Geometry

Plot the points on the coordinate system below.

1. (2, -3)

2. (-4, 1)

3. (3, 0)

4. (-1, -5)

5. (5, 6)

Use the coordinate system below to fill in the missing points.

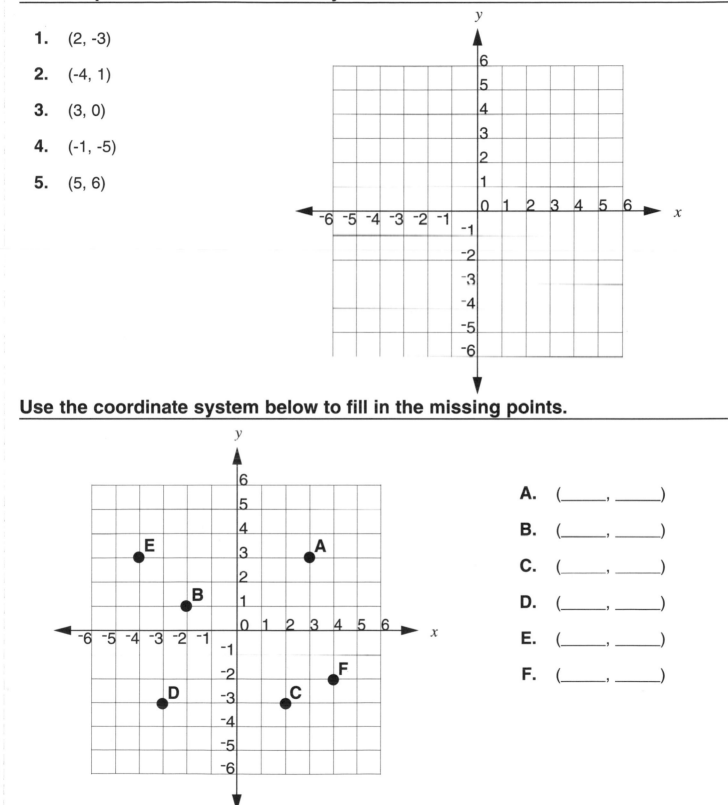

A. (_____, _____)

B. (_____, _____)

C. (_____, _____)

D. (_____, _____)

E. (_____, _____)

F. (_____, _____)

www.summerbridgeactivities.com **Math Connection—Grade 4—RBP0164**

Geometry: Lines and Angles

Remember…
Parallel lines never meet.
Perpendicular lines form a right
angle where they meet.

Draw a line parallel to each line segment below.

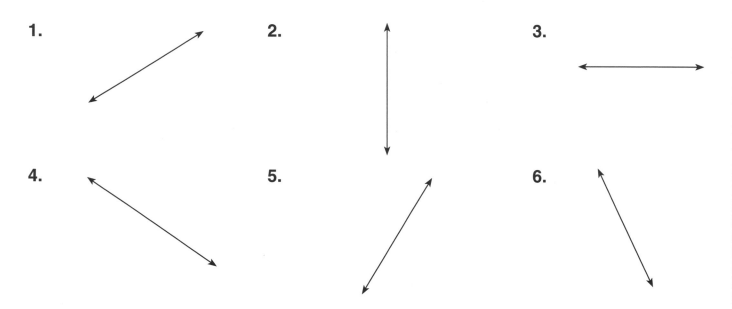

1.

2.

3.

4.

5.

6.

Draw a line perpendicular to each line segment below.

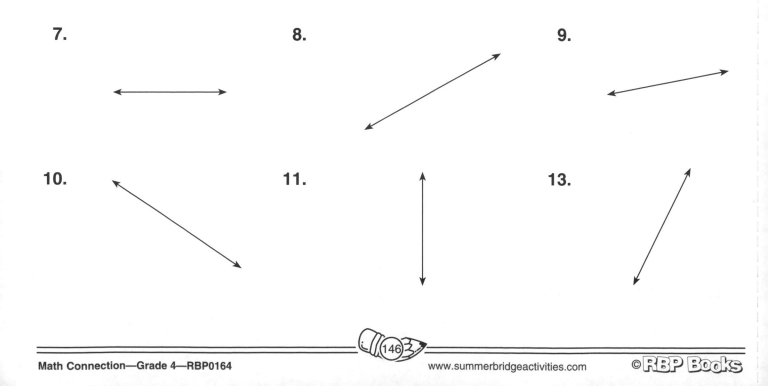

7.

8.

9.

10.

11.

13.

Geometry: Angles and Triangles

Remember...
A **scalene** triangle has **0** sides that are equal.
An **isosceles** triangle has **2** sides that are equal.
An **equilateral** triangle has **3** sides that are equal.

Write the word *scalene*, *isosceles*, or *equilateral* to describe each triangle.

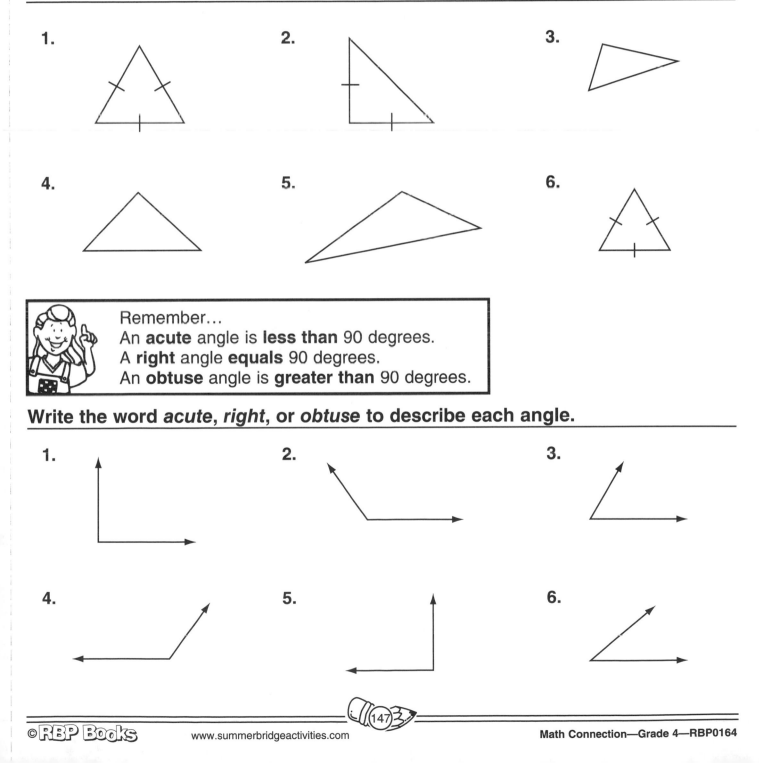

1.

2.

3.

4.

5.

6.

Remember...
An **acute** angle is **less than** 90 degrees.
A **right** angle **equals** 90 degrees.
An **obtuse** angle is **greater than** 90 degrees.

Write the word *acute*, *right*, or *obtuse* to describe each angle.

1.

2.

3.

4.

5.

6.

www.summerbridgeactivities.com   Math Connection—Grade 4—RBP0164

Real-Life Problem Solving

Solve each problem.

1.

Simon delivers newspapers. His boss told him that each customer must have a newspaper delivered by 5:30. If it takes Simon 1 hour and 15 minutes to deliver all of the papers, what time does he need to leave to deliver them?

2.

Eve is bundling newspapers. She puts 9 newspapers in each bundle. If she has 6,282 newspapers, how many bundles will she have when she's finished?

3.

Scott delivers 250 newspapers. Monica delivers 7 times as many newspapers as Eric. Eric delivers half as many newspapers as Scott. Paige and her brother deliver 12 times as many newspapers as Scott. How many papers does each person deliver?

Scott delivers: _____

Monica delivers: _____

Paige and her brother deliver:_____

Eric delivers: _____

How many newspapers are delivered altogether? _____

4.

Lindsay writes for the newspaper. The newspaper company pays 35 cents a word. If Lindsay writes a story with 5,398 words, how much money will she earn?

5.

Gary uses 2 feet of string to tie each newspaper together. If he has to tie 482 newspapers, how many **yards** of string should he buy?

6.

Jeff and his friends deliver newspapers in an area that is 17 miles by 30 miles. How many square miles does their newspaper route cover?

7.

Marcy earns $0.25 for each newspaper she sells. If she sells 136 newspapers, how much does she earn?

148

Name _____ Date _____

Real-Life Problem Solving

Kyle and his friends are shopping for their party. Use the shopping list below to solve each problem.

Shopping List

paper plates...$1.49
cups $2.59
soda (2-liter bottle) $1.19
napkins $1.15
cake $15.45
ice cream..$2.69
candy $4.75
party favors..$9.25

1.
Kyle buys 3 packages of paper plates and 4 packages of cups. How much does he spend altogether?

2.
Leslie buys 3 packages of candy. She pays with a $20.00 bill. How much change does she get back?

3.
Kathryn buys 13 2-liter bottles of soda for the party. She plans on serving 24,000 milliliters of soda. How many milliliters of soda does she have? Will she have enough soda for the party?

4.
Nicole buys 5 packages of party favors and 3 packages of candy. How much more does she spend on party favors than candy?

5.
Amy sends 135 party invitations. If she spends $0.15 to mail each invitation, how much does she spend on postage altogether?

6.
Pete buys a cake and 2 cartons of ice cream. He has 2 ten-dollar bills, 1 five-dollar bill, and 2 quarters in his wallet. How much will he have left in his wallet after he buys the items for the party?

www.summerbridgeactivities.com

© RBP Books

Math Connection—Grade 4—RBP0164

149

Real-Life Problem Solving

Solve each problem.

1.

Alice earns $2.15 an hour for babysitting. How much does she earn if she babysits for 6 hours?

2.

John takes 1 hour and 45 minutes to get to work. If he arrives to work at 8:30, what time does he leave his house?

3.

Vanessa earns $4.25 an hour for cleaning. She works 3 hours on Tuesday, 4 hours on Wednesday, and 7 hours on Saturday. How much does she earn in all?

4.

Joey spends $11.89 on baseball cards. Alex spends $13.35 on baseball cards. How much more does Alex spend than Joey?

5.

Joey buys 247 cards. He can fit 6 cards in a plastic page. How many pages will he need for all of his cards? How many cards will he have in his last page, if he fills all of the other pages?

6.

Abby buys 45 stickers for $0.25 each. She also buys 32 sheets of paper for $0.11 each. How much does she spend?

7.

Jeff earns $25.75 mowing lawns. He spends $2.66 on a pair of socks, $1.39 on some candy, and $16.77 on a CD. How much money does Jeff have left?

8.

Megan needs 252 inches of ribbon for her project. If ribbon costs $1.19 a yard, how much does she spend on ribbon?

Math Connection—Grade 4—RBP0164   www.summerbridgeactivities.com   © RBP Books

Answer Pages

Page 5
1.	4	7	17	13	14	11	15	11
2.	13	8	10	2	14	18	3	9
3.	16	10	1	12	9	15	12	18
4.	17	10	17	5	12	8	6	10
5.	7	10	8	9	11	12	14	4
6.	3	19	10	19	18	14	16	16
7.	2	13	12	10	14	16	11	17
8.	16	9	15	16	3	12	10	10
9.	6	13	9	12	20	12	14	14
10.	9	9	7	21	7	15	19	7

Page 6
1.	11	8	4	13	5	12	15	9
2.	15	4	15	7	13	16	7	10
3.	3	9	4	10	14	12	9	12
4.	7	7	18	3	20	14	9	10
5.	11	5	11	11	6	2	8	14
6.	10	14	16	11	14	19	11	16
7.	5	11	9	8	10	13	14	11
8.	15	8	6	18	6	12	16	10
9.	6	20	10	15	12	7	16	14
10.	11	15	17	6	8	10	21	19

Page 7
1.	10	6	4	6	10	3	5	1
2.	0	9	10	5	11	8	10	3
3.	4	7	0	7	7	2	6	1
4.	10	10	9	9	3	8	2	3
5.	9	4	7	0	5	1	9	4
6.	1	8	7	9	8	2	0	8
7.	8	9	9	2	6	8	8	9
8.	5	7	3	4	6	8	7	5
9.	2	5	7	4	7	2	7	1
10.	8	2	6	7	1	3	3	4

Page 8
1.	2	4	0	3	6	6	6	11
2.	0	4	1	1	1	6	6	1
3.	2	0	9	9	1	5	0	7
4.	5	5	10	1	10	8	3	3
5.	8	5	7	5	2	8	9	3
6.	2	1	6	7	4	0	1	3
7.	5	3	7	8	10	9	9	4
8.	5	3	8	7	5	2	1	4
9.	4	3	8	0	2	1	6	6
10.	0	6	7	4	7	2	9	0

Page 9
1.	0	35	45	64	6	35	16	56
2.	4	8	12	1	48	15	30	0
3.	21	0	8	9	81	6	63	48
4.	12	20	27	5	28	0	18	7
5.	3	56	20	50	54	25	16	42
6.	10	36	72	7	0	72	2	80
7.	0	12	0	63	6	24	15	0
8.	70	18	3	42	54	30	14	4
9.	24	8	32	60	0	36	20	24
10.	0	45	35	18	40	4	49	40

Page 10
1.	10	7	9	10	90	21	49	28
2.	8	48	12	56	63	48	25	18
3.	55	42	8	32	0	8	16	40
4.	16	14	24	5	54	72	16	9
5.	72	3	30	56	12	36	42	4
6.	63	40	81	24	21	44	18	70
7.	40	36	80	14	0	27	15	0
8.	36	12	32	24	90	45	64	27
9.	30	28	20	10	45	60	35	18
10.	0	54	33	35	0	4	66	30

Page 11
1.	7	9	2	6	6
2.	3	5	1	8	1
3.	4	5	3	1	9
4.	5	7	2	5	5
5.	8	3	1	2	2
6.	6	9	0	6	4
7.	9	4	1	10	8
8.	12	6	4	7	7
9.	5	9	5	8	9
10.	6	11	4	9	8

Page 12
1.	1	2	2	9	1
2.	8	1	1	10	9
3.	9	8	7	9	3
4.	2	9	1	3	7
5.	3	3	3	3	9
6.	8	6	4	7	7
7.	9	4	4	3	10
8.	7	5	4	5	5
9.	5	7	11	5	4
10.	6	5	10	8	10

Page 17
1.	56	77	29	88	47	95
2.	69	25	14	82	16	88
3.	39	77	77	99	67	98
4.	89	49	97	92	89	108
5.	13	22	93	64	42	31
6.	80	42	64	72	91	43
7.	10	20	50	10	40	20
8.	6	41	33	27	40	33

www.summerbridgeactivities.com

Math Connection—Grade 4—RBP0164

Answer Pages

Page 18
1. 95 59 29 69 56 18
2. 17 29 87 39 48 98
3. 47 65 18 94 19 34
4. 13 41 63 85 61 26
5. 31 52 72 32 21 12
6. 10 93 51 42 63 32

Page 19
1. 75 87 36 99 69 39
2. 29 98 79 58 38 18
3. 30 90 90 90 80 100
4. 70 80 80 90 70 80
5. 34 39 89 67 46 79
6. 67 99 78 97 98 89
7. 59 58 89 98 49 99

Page 20
1. 4 1 2 4 3 2
2. 27 42 34 12 21 12
3. 34 42 30 52 62 86
4. 30 20 50 20 10 10
5. 40 20 20 20 10 20
6. 16 3 41 26 3 11
7. 55 12 25 33 22 23

Page 21
1. 18 38 29 56 47 18
2. 25 47 37 56 19 98
3. 32 89 89 77 86 59
4. 89 57 77 67 89 94
5. 23 16 33 53 12 45
6. 20 30 20 20 40 20
7. 33 21 11 2 3 23
8. 43 41 2 15 16 72

Page 22
1. 17 27 38 49 57 67
2. 28 49 39 58 67 79
3. 50 90 80 90 90 80
4. 68 69 76 89 69 98
5. 31 47 20 72 32 27
6. 50 50 20 50 20 40
7. 31 13 24 2 52 22
8. 24 33 47 27 43 57

Page 23
1. 28 hamsters　2. 14 rabbits
3. 13 goldfish　4. 38 pounds
5. 31 fish　6. 51 ants
7. 44 insects　8. 19 reptiles

Page 24
1. 56 points　2. 39 points　3. 27 points
4. 28 points　5. 38 points　6. 96 points
7. 76 baskets　8. 27 points

Page 25
1. 18 29 37 67 97 48
2. 48 16 69 57 17 75
3. 37 68 89 69 99 128
4. 77 89 78 76 99 89
5. 21 12 33 54 64 52
6. 41 72 13 24 52 96
7. 2 14 13 33 12 21
8. 36 51 60 63 42 41

Page 26
triangle 3 3 3
quadrilateral 4 4 4
pentagon 5 5 5
hexagon 6 6 6
heptagon 7 7 7
octagon 8 8 8

Page 27
1. 10 9 11 13 7 14
2. 53 20 73 62 41 82
3. 55 84 124 112 104 127
4. 133 120 148 96 117 112
5. 9 19 32 79 45 55
6. 9 14 35 28 24 27
7. 135 306 516 784 625 684
8. 816 434 382 358 356 89

Page 28
1. 31 24 40 25 31 41
2. 54 32 91 43 23 35
3. 74 72 91 43 81 80
4. 34 83 83 56 80 74
5. 93 92 80 95 92 93
6. 54 73 95 55 44 85
7. 84 74 85 84 102 98

Page 29
1. 14 17 11 16 16 21
2. 20 21 18 25 20 18
3. 81 79 74 83 83 51
4. 78 106 95 107 90 101
5. 168 126 249 145 178 209
6. 177 208 179 209 147 169

Math Connection—Grade 4—RBP0164　www.summerbridgeactivities.com　© RBP Books

Answer Pages

Page 30
1.	94	146	111	139	161	111
2.	120	172	114	106	135	105
3.	153	134	113	115	142	182
4.	112	101	113	124	142	122
5.	182	195	242	171	191	222
6.	186	211	185	219	159	177
7.	136	226	180	177	198	156

Page 31
1.	7	28	56	16	38	56
2.	48	25	54	15	6	36
3.	45	15	18	19	47	8
4.	9	3	7	56	28	36
5.	38	17	9	14	37	36
6.	224	319	234	415	818	657

Page 32
1.	67	161	124	69	282	567
2.	425	195	288	384	591	891
3.	183	792	593	455	872	342
4.	279	587	399	569	927	58
5.	52	345	615	132	487	711
6.	560	467	65	319	904	673

Page 33
1.	152	154	186	275	304	918
2.	979	708	464	900	841	666
3.	129	227	191	248	138	162
4.	130	189	169	229	145	239
5.	7	53	25	9	18	17
6.	612	409	219	802	614	718
7.	201	665	518	576	289	822
8.	399	65	859	678	189	509

Page 34
1.	22	20	17	14	18	19
2.	100	77	46	33	75	61
3.	124	74	127	112	115	131
4.	179	158	101	134	146	91
5.	18	57	26	49	69	84
6.	18	15	6	24	6	18
7.	43	8	8	29	16	36
8.	137	355	525	657	203	713

Page 35
1. 39 reptiles
2. 77 pictures
3. 802 pounds
4. 1,236 pounds
5. 81 reptiles
6. 243 people
7. 170 cages
8. 262 feet

Page 36
1. 79 stickers
2. 73 marbles
3. 89 cards
4. 383 office supplies
5. 76 stamps
6. 82 pieces
7. $133.20
8. $60.07

Page 37
1.	41	35	60	28	81	57
2.	94	111	132	171	121	183
3.	412	640	271	332	756	935
4.	108	144	220	174	225	175
5.	28	39	47	18	17	14
6.	534	332	133	418	236	833
7.	561	627	857	161	459	745

Page 38
1. 11 marbles   2. 5 marbles
3. 5/11   4. 3/11   5. 1/11
6. 2/11   7. 0/11   8. 3/11

Page 39
1.	1,078	500	1,051	337	868	1,423
2.	11,206	7,454	10,560	9,712	16,596	6,547
3.	133	151	2,370	2,296	14,033	11,896
4.	93	89	1,064	952	6,605	9,168
5.	151	210	309	502	615	286
6.	1,109	3,293	4,822	2,308	3,212	8,286
7.	1,215	5,284	1,109	1,701	3,675	259
8.	34,123	1,108	42,168	21,192	48,131	91,781

Page 40
1.	993	790	929	1,377	1,117	1,291
2.	922	805	1,238	1,131	1,041	615
3.	535	1,337	1,451	1,362	1,066	1,598
4.	435	409	222	184	88	
5.	1,217	1,541	522	617	1,770	
6.	1,363	2,438	1,640	2,079	849	
7.	601	1,088	981	779	3,062	

Page 41
1.	1,919	4,002	7,183	5,294	2,560	6,231
2.	4,892	2,102	11,493	11,520	9,382	6,235
3.	12,268	13,300	7,669	5,977	11,686	10,721
4.	2,913	2,073	7,233	6,209	1,818	
5.	1,319	718	718	4,788	2,088	
6.	24,308	59,329	52,326	31,741	33,854	

Page 42
1.	49	67	71	135	128
2.	279	396	192	694	394
3.	785	988	678	983	935
4.	12,796	14,398	13,499	12,217	10,875
5.	8,388	6,617	7,729	8,026	11,307
6.	8,576	12,404	12,231	10,843	11,584

Page 43
1.	60	71	116	148	122
2.	419	239	348	675	537
3.	674	910	1,165	1,337	1,071
4.	9,511	10,012	7,704	17,396	7,983
5.	9,512	14,169	7,200	14,455	13,940
6.	27,189	45,986	62,245	51,389	72,505

www.summerbridgeactivities.com   Math Connection—Grade 4—RBP0164

Answer Pages

Page 44
1. 574 | 382 | 873 | 1,458 | 1,478
2. 3,012 | 7,025 | 4,651 | 1,988 | 4,739
3. 10,401 | 15,838 | 12,039 | 6,503 | 13,291
4. 7,844 | 15,888 | 1,208 | 1,539 | 14,186
5. 122 | 81 | 372 | 23 | 377
6. 3,248 | 4,700 | 6,846 | 3,386 | 5,882
7. 5,330 | 4,921 | 1,929 | 3,069 | 2,633
8. 85,208 | 38,963 | 51,272 | 31,916 | 11,735

Page 45
1. 2,709 red yo-yos 2. 678 stickers
3. 1,069 marbles 4. 1,343 feet
5. 7,856 toys 6. 1,713 inches
7. 1,893 people 8. $16.25

Page 46
1. 434 black ants 2. 1,292 pounds
3. 553 feet 4. 1,078 butterflies
5. 46,084 insects 6. 10,176 birds
7. 1,785 insects 8. 957 butterflies

Page 47
1. 595 | 606 | 416 | 3,934 | 7,505
2. 4,895 | 8,258 | 5,736 | 6,338 | 35,298
3. 177 | 158 | 146 | 466 | 19,287
4. 495 | 828 | 395 | 1,389 | 14,538
5. 412 | 172 | 183 | 346 | 221
6. 1,602 | 2,157 | 2,849 | 30,646 | 49,218

Page 48
1. 24 | 99 2. 27 | 12
3. 3,520 | 45 4. 6 | 7,040
5. 81 | 72 6. 1 | 144
7. 1 | 2 8. 135 | 5
9. 9 | 36 10. 48 | 2
11. 3 | 36 12. 3 | 5,280
13. 120 | 24 14. 8 | 96

Page 49
1. 48 | 99 2. 36 | 16
3. 5,280 | 21 4. 7 | 3
5. 108 | 8 6. 3 | 7
7. 2 miles 8. 21 feet 9. 9 feet
10. 4 yards 11. 9 yards 12. 3 miles

Page 50
1. 5 miles 2. 2 yards 3. 5 yards 4. 3 miles
5. 27 feet 6. 71 inches 7. 5 miles 8. 7 yards

Page 51
1. 26 | 77 | 96 | 48 | 60 | 62
2. 48 | 60 | 44 | 48 | 126 | 66
3. 32 | 84 | 76 | 87 | 96 | 85
4. 210 | 66 | 200 | 33 | 560 | 90
5. 168 | 387 | 342 | 152 | 230 | 208
6. 260 | 900 | 404 | 1,200 | 1,008 | 248
7. 624 | 838 | 2,052 | 1,694 | 326 | 1,557
8. 4,810 | 310 | 1,935 | 2,616 | 1,557 | 6,517
9. 3,829 | 7,839 | 2,740 | 2,892 | 2,748 | 891

Page 52
1. 6 | 60 | 4 | 40 | 7 | 70
2. 8 | 84 | 9 | 93 | 4 | 44
3. 63 | 28 | 66 | 48 | 48 | 68
4. 99 | 93 | 99 | 48 | 88 | 46
5. 39 | 48 | 46 | 80 | 66 | 28
6. 48 | 22 | 63 | 84 | 24 | 39
7. 55 | 12 | 80 | 80 | 99 | 80

Page 53
1. 28 | 66 | 36 | 44 | 70 | 63
2. 189 | 26 | 355 | 96 | 147 | 104
3. 183 | 48 | 93 | 328 | 124 | 300
4. 99 | 246 | 99 | 48 | 560 | 88
5. 39 | 48 | 46 | 80 | 66 | 28
6. 270 | 88 | 204 | 48 | 216 | 320
7. 88 | 106 | 180 | 33 | 486 | 126

Page 54
1. 270 | 228 | 66 | 765 | 310 | 92
2. 531 | 205 | 392 | 450 | 196 | 78
3. 228 | 189 | 516 | 336 | 122 | 285
4. 406 | 384 | 215 | 279 | 680 | 312
5. 882 | 288 | 413 | 96 | 476 | 752
6. 420 | 301 | 504 | 168 | 219 | 180
7. 1,602 | 1,860 | 394 | 858 | 5,157 | 3,128

Page 55
1. 105 | 96 | 88 | 82 | 26 | 68
2. 38 | 72 | 70 | 94 | 144 | 108
3. 216 | 162 | 114 | 581 | 152 | 260
4. 738 | 371 | 194 | 196 | 232 | 380
5. 465 | 444 | 595 | 177 | 372 | 188
6. 462 | 366 | 644 | 840 | 824 | 360
7. 354 | 436 | 916 | 814 | 705 | 692
8. 368 | 984 | 1,168 | 706 | 1,524 | 1,386
9. 2,628 | 1,488 | 2,140 | 2,613 | 3,976 | 2,436

Page 56
1. 62 | 88 | 33 | 93 | 99 | 60
2. 64 | 26 | 48 | 84 | 44 | 140
3. 255 | 98 | 108 | 438 | 147 | 80
4. 140 | 310 | 144 | 498 | 224 | 630
5. 248 | 736 | 318 | 504 | 320 | 465
6. 842 | 336 | 408 | 214 | 628 | 844
7. 645 | 381 | 1,456 | 838 | 987 | 296
8. 2,600 | 1,743 | 1,168 | 926 | 1,524 | 1,960
9. 2,610 | 5,096 | 1,152 | 4,032 | 1,390 | 914

Math Connection—Grade 4—RBP0164   www.summerbridgeactivities.com   ©RBP Books

Answer Pages

Page 57
1. 3,372 miles
2. 3,215 miles
3. 2,241 miles
4. 3,156 miles
5. 2,082 miles
6. 815 miles
7. 455 miles
8. Tony: 2,911 miles, Paul: 2,368

Page 58
1. 1,316 miles
2. 60 miles
3. 784 hours
4. 288 marshmallows
5. 1,098 yards
6. 1,498 campers
7. 1,368 ounces
8. 348 pictures

Page 59
1.	55	48	63	82	80	93
2.	48	90	66	69	88	66
3.	72	87	108	84	104	240
4.	210	426	252	153	126	78
5.	456	238	208	448	222	285
6.	280	690	448	780	856	372
7.	512	658	1,696	1,296	519	1,173
8.	3,290	924	3,504	1,395	2,961	3,220
9.	1,270	5,288	3,220	2,562	5,808	2,112

Page 60
1. 8:45
2. 10:15
3. 8:15
4. 10:45
5. 10:45
6. 11:45
7. 12:00
8. 1:45

9. 2:20 P.M.
10. 9:55 P.M.
11. 7:20 A.M.
12. 10:00 P.M.

Page 61
1.	630	680	850	1,240	2,580	2,250
2.	806	336	325	828	3,066	1,176
3.	5,481	14,880	66,674	10,640	6,160	47,360
4.	18,054	8,928	14,832	30,012	26,062	14,516
5.	14,924	34,440	11,680	23,655	11,466	9,360

Page 62
1.	24	240	104	1,040	126	1,260
2.	48	480	108	1,080	115	1,150
3.	124	1,240	64	640	205	2,050
4.	248	2,480	243	2,430	42	420

Page 63
1.	28	280	108	1,080	135	1,350
2.	72	1,032	57	437	90	810
3.	186	2,666	513	1,083	135	1,215
4.	567	2,997	160	2,080	564	2,444

Page 64
1.	74	444	256	2,176	72	1,992
2.	312	768	264	414	1,768	1,032
3.	408	1,271	345	714	689	204
4.	1,302	350	800	357	385	338
5.	870	1,088	4,200	1,005	2,173	1,197

Page 65
1.	1,530	3,040	780	3,120	6,720	3,720
2.	966	408	473	736	1,353	585
3.	1,008	2,914	2,523	1,972	1,197	2,888
4.	1,305	5,766	612	2,548	1,152	4,623

Page 66
1.	1,280	370	4,480	570	4,350	6,440
2.	450	1,984	636	1,426	1,380	608
3.	1,302	2,268	3,283	900	1,482	666
4.	1,472	868	1,254	1,722	5,146	817
5.	1,215	1,881	1,020	1,444	5,037	6,794

Page 67
1.	438	4,380	2,044	20,440	2,534	25,340
2.	250	1,500	1,620	11,340	1,255	11,295
3.	4,064	29,043	5,992	21,033	9,824	
4.	6,156	34,290	15,085	19,521	12,825	

Page 68
1.	1,623	16,230	438	4,380	3,858	38,580
2.	914	14,624	801	11,481	4,075	52,975
3.	6,935	11,934	23,364	8,338	9,513	
4.	40,979	15,048	34,358	21,276	61,128	
5.	15,561	11,956	43,513	51,992	12,936	

Page 69
1.	744	1,440	1,824	3,807	2,204	5,103
2.	2,028	3,185	1,998	2,392	2,592	3,276
3.	2,397	2,808	2,262	612	817	3,380
4.	10,578	14,712	25,251	34,998	38,684	
5.	6,864	65,436	16,031	9,744	78,556	

Page 70
1.	760	1,909	1,488	4,307	2,470	636
2.	5,340	1,222	558	2,054	2,914	2,028
3.	12,096	43,746	25,205	15,665	62,580	25,821
4.	11,280	17,907	8,132	45,507	58,044	33,323
5.	28,025	24,990	59,150	9,193	10,245	14,212

Page 71
1. 703 people
2. $474.81
3. 5,772 people
4. 5,292 miles
5. 336 people
6. $32,838
7. $61.92
8. 570 minutes

Page 72
1. 4,263 raspberries
2. 360 seeds
3. 5,922 sq. ft.
4. 450 bags
5. 8,881 sq. ft.
6. 705 plants
7. 4,752 peaches
8. 804 flowers

www.summerbridgeactivities.com Math Connection—Grade 4—RBP0164

Page 73
1.	870	2,700	380	4,340	5,220
2.	1,333	338	1,944	4,473	1,025
3.	2,542	592	2,407	1,943	2,544
4.	24,672	10,668	28,602	30,609	26,928
5.	25,064	30,723	15,312	43,416	8,853

Page 74
1.	12	15	18	21
2.	32	64	128	256
3.	25	30	35	40
4.	34	30	26	22
5.	30	37	44	51
6.	100,000	1,000,000	10,000,000	100,000,000
7.	30	36	42	48
8.	10	12	14	16

Page 75
1.	4,286	4,128	36,218	16,320
2.	170,753	143,594	426,024	698,196
3.	615,307	89,964	216,597	190,464
4.	2,653,884	3,369,289	1,573,351	5,684,461
5.	14,448,652	18,351,936	5,714,334	13,656,360

Page 76
1.	6,000	9,000	8,440	6,042	12,630
2.	6,290	8,164	30,720	13,628	25,563
3.	25,084	59,024	10,358	45,170	14,716
4.	9,723	13,944	35,884	9,618	68,838
5.	16,824	38,540	33,580	22,074	21,176

Page 77
1.	6,000	60,000	36,000	360,000
2.	150,000	240,000	210,000	320,000
3.	124,148	124,499	34,160	148,274
4.	506,678	86,336	187,124	187,145
5.	496,098	401,822	277,204	96,588

Page 78
1.	54,015	105,315	31,600	108,281
2.	151,152	103,077	41,340	354,312
3.	83,390	71,526	272,748	47,664
4.	486,972	96,012	29,792	317,952
5.	96,516	185,742	260,451	499,058

Page 79
1.	23,200	78,600	436,800	224,400
2.	63,612	69,120	39,804	108,468
3.	85,902	43,896	110,808	251,526
4.	665,808	151,985	3,486,294	671,922
5.	2,647,359	795,906	645,456	1,662,768

Page 80
1.	45,010	68,442	50,743	262,122
2.	62,272	374,072	43,320	218,435
3.	698,544	1,817,728	1,045,682	2,904,048
4.	15,966,588	2,693,052	11,360,331	23,640,064

Page 81
Allison: 2,424   Max: 1,212
Jeff: 36,360   Caroline: 27,876
Greg: 26,278   Julie: 26,624
Becky: 840,896

Page 82
1. 16,945 people   2. 20,730 rubber balls
3. 25,560 gallons of red punch
4. $739.75   5. $12,006
6. 7,428 people
7. 135,296 pints of vanilla ice cream
8. 219,696 balloons

Page 83
1.	9,345	37,812	18,344	25,630
2.	77,511	66,638	226,044	294,735
3.	135,135	85,232	335,988	199,080
4.	1,372,168	2,447,025	311,542	4,603,005
5.	2,013,714	7,984,693	3,753,501	29,095,192

Page 84
1. $6.35   2. $9.27   3. $4.42   4. $5.75
5. $7.61   6. $3.84   7. $15.22   8. $24.34
9. $57.19   10. $70.99   11. $35.29   12. $85.15
13. $1.00   14. $1.07   15. $5.17   16. $15.53
17. $60.62   18. $1.50

Page 85
1.	$1.01	$0.46	$0.46	$0.48	$0.42
2.	$9.19	$8.27	$1.50	$1.54	$8.89
3.	$5.88	$7.10	$5.10	$1.40	$8.56
4.	$7.65	$8.55	$7.72	$10.31	$2.55
5.	$8.87	$7.99	$1.05	$4.05	$8.66
6.	$96.86	$30.66	$8.17	$19.01	$117.20

Page 86
1.	$1.30	$2.80	$4.71	$79.80	$408.95
2.	$3.84	$55.80	$13.50	$97.75	$120.45
3.	$4,157.32	$170.50	$1,432.20	$26,239.78	$9,229.25
4.	$7.50				
5.	$6.32				
6.	$17.43				
7.	$517.35				

Answer Pages

Page 87
1. 8 2 5 2 7
2. 4 0 1 5 9
3. 3 8 9 7 6
4. 6 4 6 7 4
5. 9 2 9 5 9
6. 5 8 7 8 2
7. 3 1 9 7 9
8. 6 7 4 2 3
9. 6 7 8 8 6
10. 6 0 1 4 5

Page 88
1. 3 3 2 7
2. 0 5 6 3
3. 6 5 2 9
4. 3 8 5 7
5. 4 4 7 8
6. 2 7 3 6
7. 4 5 4 8

Page 89
1. 9 5 4 8
2. 9 4 8 5
3. 6 8 7 7
4. 9 5 9 7
5. 4 4 0 8 2
6. 7 9 8 4 9
7. 4 7 8 6 3

Page 90
1. 7 6 2 7
2. 8 3 4 8
3. 7 7 6 0
4. 6 8 6 5
5. 6 8 7 3 8
6. 5 8 9 7 4
7. 5 4 0 5 2
8. 9 6 3 2 2

Page 91
1. 4 sheets   2. 6 bottles
3. 6 packages   4. 7 boxes
5. 6 cartons   6. 8 packages
7. 7 sheets   8. 7 boxes, $1.00

Page 92
1. 9 packages   2. 5 cartons
3. $4   4. $11
5. 7 packages with 3 left over
6. 5 bottles   7. 4 bags
8. 8 pounds

Page 93
1. 8 5 4 8 9
2. 4 7 1 9 6
3. 5 7 9 3 6
4. 0 9 2 9 4
5. 6 3 3 2 7
6. 0 7 4 2 8
7. 8 2 4 4 9
8. 1 9 7 4 8
9. 7 gumdrops   10. 8 chocolates

Page 94
1. 75° F   15° F   40° F
2. 65° C   40° C   35° C
3. 105° F   80° F   10° F
4. 15° C   20° C   55° C

Page 95
1. 19 R2   7 R5   12 R4   13 R1   13 R5
2. 65 R1   6 R6   2 R6   49   32 R1
3. 9 R1   29   8 R3   15   33 R1
4. 24   204   141   63   38 R7
5. 78 R6   181 R2   32   19 R3   71 R2

Page 96
1. 14   13   21   8   11
2. 12   10   12   12   13
3. 14   14   16   14   14
4. 15   13   13   10   15
5. 14   11   15   16   12

Page 97
1. 13 R2   7 R1   12 R1   11 R4   8 R2
2. 7 R1   7 R1   22 R1   17 R1   6 R6
3. 17 R1   17 R1   21 R2   9 R2   13 R2
4. 14   33 R1   8 R2   19   17 R4

Page 98
1. 22 R3   9 R1   39   7 R4   18
2. 3 R1   14 R4   9 R5   24 R1   28
3. 8 R3   15 R1   19 R1   49   11 R1
4. 11 R7   12 R2   18 R1   7 R2   7 R3

Page 99
1. 56   27   65   87   82
2. 27   69   91   47   78
3. 92   142   191   63   82
4. 28   43   96   97   24
5. 23   87   84   68   58

Page 100
1. 327   134 R1   321 R1   117 R1   154 R1
2. 168   106 R1   40 R7   140 R1   146
3. 108   152 R5   207 R1   196 R1   158 R1
4. 252 R1   13 R4   75 R1   23 R8   161 R4
5. 80 R7   107 R2   200 R1   90 R2   124 R2

Page 101

1. 492 R1	62 R1	15 R7	35 R4	132 R3
2. 128	137	13 R6	236 R3	12 R6
3. 90 R1	66 R1	126 R2	30 R3	40 R4
4. 244 R1	29 R6	476	102 R2	224 R2
5. 118 R3	288 R2	57 R5	305 R2	112 R4

Page 102

1. 19	30 R1	17 R1	8 R2	17 R1
2. 12 R1	24 R1	8 R2	5 R3	15 R4
3. 78	84 R2	165 R2	101 R2	338 R1
4. 92 R5	108 R1	47	203 R1	27
5. 92	91	27	63	67 R1

Page 103

1. 15 snakes   **2.** 79 pounds
3. 83 pounds   **4.** 210 people
5. 13 customers   **6.** 15 pounds with 5 pounds left over
7. 260 people   **8.** 63 pounds

Page 104

1. 39 boxes   **2.** 8 feet
3. 91 degrees F   **4.** 55 degrees F
5. 47 feet   **6.** 13 inches
7. 15 inches   **8.** 74 boxes with 2 shovels left over

Page 105

1. 22 R1	32	12 R1	1 R6	17 R2
2. 9 R4	14 R1	9 R1	8 R3	29 R1
3. 65	69	82	82	87
4. 99	89	28	67	26
5. 104 R5	275 R1	82 R3	11 R1	122 R2

Page 106

1. 3,000   8   14   **2.** 84   9,000   41
3. 73,000   57   25   **4.** 7   12,000   118
5. 6   2   65,000   **6.** 4 g
7. 15,000 mg   **8.** 2,000 g   **9.** 16 g

Page 107

1. 50   7   8   **2.** 16   6   360
3. 4   2,000   1,500   **4.** 9   7,200   4,000
5. 900   5   840   **6.** 17,000   30   6,100
7. 3,000; m 7,000 m   **8.** Kayla

Page 108

1. 8,000   5   15,000   **2.** 48   4,000   33
3. 92,000   21,000   7   **4.** 6,000   8   7,000
5. 18 L   **6.** 500 mL
7. 14,000 mL   **8.** 12 liters left, 6 2-liter bottles

Page 109

1. 103	31	259	21	91
2. 412	154 R1	1,214	192 R4	1,124
3. 325	1,717 R3	1,183 R7	966	812 R4
4. 3,157	637	221	1,519 R2	1,079 R4

Page 110

1. 98	63	29	54	66
2. 75	36	95	77	48
3. 88	63	49	85	23

Page 111

1. 87 R1	37 R6	109 R1	178 R4	126
2. 462	142 R2	37 R1	61 R1	189 R2
3. 30 R3	236 R3	122 R3	151 R1	82 R1
4. 124 R5	485 R1	111 R1	99 R5	53 R2

Page 112

1. 1,241	402	599	654	204
2. 714 R1	922 R3	1,028 R2	4,308 R1	931 R1

Page 113

1. 88	72	89	43	88
2. 99	22	25	74	201
3. 103	55	54	38	212
4. 3,091	421	624	361	243
5. 225 R6	1,194 R1	1,630 R1	562 R2	2,109 R1

Page 114

1. 234	75	22 R3	130 R1	135 R2
2. 50 R4	66 R3	47	463	197 R2
3. 164 R3	35 R1	18 R5	96	41 R3
4. 237 R1	1,630 R2	1,330 R1	1,213 R3	917 R3

Page 115

1. 89	421 R1	39 R4	194 R3	122 R1
2. 66 R3	99 R6	139 R1	72 R3	14 R3
3. 101 R6	137 R2	30 R4	180 R2	31 R3
4. 3,357 R1	1,177 R1	1,068 R5	419	1,375 R3

Page 116

1. 420 R2	804	213 R1	402 R4	706 R2
2. 447 R3	508 R1	2,169	2,454 R1	614 R5
3. 4,736 R1	1,623 R3	1,146 R5	1,194 R1	301 R8
4. 316 R3	1,598 R1	1,103 R2	180 R3	1,544 R3

Page 117

1. 218	51	167 R2	114 R5	63 R1
2. 414 R3	418 R2	246 R3	739 R6	815
3. 1,318 R1	680 R2	1,354 R1	309	1,293 R4
4. 811 R4	368	215 R4	972	3,004 R2

Page 118
1. 82 R5   64   51 R2   46 R4   113
2. 503 R1   2,812 R1   692   1,022 R3   441 R3
3. 564 R6   936 R2   1,895 R4   2,118   2,293
4. 3,335 R1   856   432   1,893 R1   439 R1

Page 119
1. 215 cartons   2. 801 boxes
3. 1,330 packages with 5 seeds left over
4. 811 bottles   5. 48 boxes
6. 405 vases with 2 flowers left over
7. 398 bottles
8. 306 packages with 1 piece of fruit left over

Page 120
1. 636 miles   2. 72 pictures
3. 392 tourists   4. 79 rows
5. 66 miles   6. 1,696 passengers
7. 91 customers   8. 950 miles

Page 121
1. 128 R2   89   61   135 R2   339
2. 905 R1   1,835 R3   607 R2   601 R6   729 R3
3. 742   1,614 R1   1,343 R1   987   352 R1
4. 353 R5   1,216 R6   742 R1   552   912

Page 122
1. 63   47   55
2. 376   985   282
3. 899   967   884

Page 123
1. 104 R3   318 R2   83 R1
2. 1,297 R2   563 R8   788 R5
3. 988 R7   418 R3   1,846 R1

Page 124
1. 107   91 R2   154 R2
2. 88   90 R5   166 R1
3. 1,349 R5   1,074   644
4. 914 R5   655 R1   901 R1

Page 125
1. 32 in.   2. 25 cm   3. 58 yd.   4. 32 m
5. 24 cm   6. 41 m   7. 40 in.   8. 76 ft.

Page 126
1. 24 ft.   2. 35 cm   3. 280 m   4. 310 in.
5. 120 in.   6. 336 in.   7. 146 ft.   8. 55 in.

Page 127
1. 2,008 in.   2. 106 ft.   3. 206 ft.   4. 398 in.
5. 13 ft.   6. 90 ft.   7. 108 m   8. 8 yd.

Page 128
1. 81 sq. in.   2. 36 sq. cm   3. 60 sq. ft.   4. 77 sq. m
5. 78 sq. m   6. 48 sq. m   7. 90 sq. yd.   8. 16 sq. ft.

Page 129
1. 28 sq. in.   2. 64 sq. m   3. 80 sq. m   4. 25 sq. cm
5. 420 sq. m   6. 975 sq. in.   7. 54 sq. yd.   8. 495 sq. ft.

Page 130
1. 384 sq. ft.   2. 1,421 sq. in.
3. 36 sq. ft.   4. 672 sq. in.
5. 972 sq. in.   6. 4 yd. 6 in.
7. 4 packages   8. 3 gallons

Page 131
1. 2   72   24   2. 6   5,280   15
3. 48   9   5   4. 2   18   60
5. 84   10   7,040
6. 14 yd.   7. 4 yd.
8. 18 ft.   9. 66 in.

Page 132
1. 6   6   9   2. 4   15   16
3. 27   7   14   4. 20   2   6
5. 28   9   12   6. 16 pints
7. 6 tablespoons   8. 32 servings
9. 2 quarts

Page 133
1. 8   10   64   2. 28   12   17
3. 64   8   36   4. 30   30   44
5. 2   12   7
6. 14 pints   7. 24 cups
8. 7 gallons   9. 116 bottles

Page 134
1. 2   35   108   2. 2   480   7
3. 2   5   63   4. 300   180   2,400
5. 84   42   4   6. 28 days
7. 4 weeks   8. 8 hours
9. 10 hours, 30 minutes

Page 135
1. $\frac{5}{6}$ 2. $\frac{1}{8}$ 3. $\frac{2}{3}$ 4. $\frac{4}{8}$
5. $\frac{16}{32}$ 6. $\frac{3}{12}$ 7. $\frac{2}{5}$ 8. $\frac{3}{8}$

Page 136
1. >   2. >   3. >   4. =
5. >   6. <   7. >   8. >
9. <   10. =   11. =   12. <
13. <   14. <   15. =   16. <

Page 137
1. $\frac{2}{2}$, 1   2. $\frac{11}{6}$, $1\frac{5}{6}$ 3. $\frac{6}{5}$, $1\frac{1}{5}$ 4. $\frac{7}{3}$, $2\frac{1}{3}$
5. $\frac{11}{4}$, $2\frac{3}{4}$ 6. $\frac{17}{6}$, $2\frac{5}{6}$

   www.summerbridgeactivities.com   Math Connection—Grade 4—RBP0164

Answer Pages

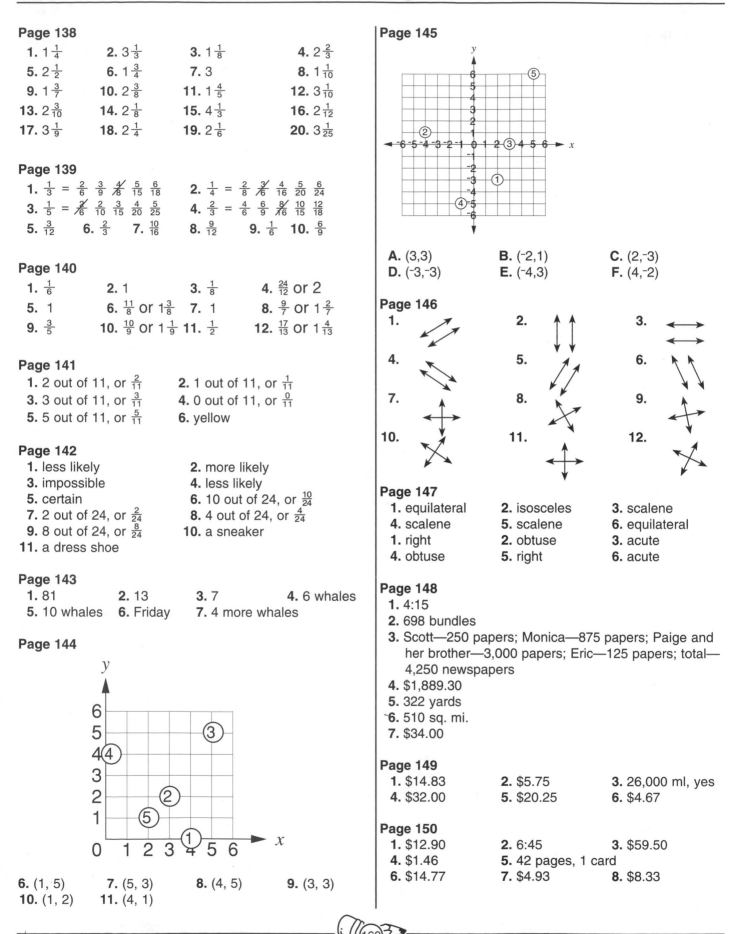

Page 138
1. $1\frac{1}{4}$　　2. $3\frac{1}{3}$　　3. $1\frac{1}{8}$　　4. $2\frac{2}{3}$
5. $2\frac{1}{2}$　　6. $1\frac{3}{4}$　　7. 3　　8. $1\frac{1}{10}$
9. $1\frac{3}{7}$　　10. $2\frac{3}{8}$　　11. $1\frac{4}{5}$　　12. $3\frac{1}{10}$
13. $2\frac{3}{10}$　　14. $2\frac{1}{8}$　　15. $4\frac{1}{3}$　　16. $2\frac{1}{12}$
17. $3\frac{1}{9}$　　18. $2\frac{1}{4}$　　19. $2\frac{1}{6}$　　20. $3\frac{1}{25}$

Page 139
1. $\frac{1}{3} = \frac{2}{6}\ \frac{3}{9}\ \cancel{\frac{4}{8}}\ \frac{5}{15}\ \frac{6}{18}$　　2. $\frac{1}{4} = \frac{2}{8}\ \cancel{\frac{3}{16}}\ \frac{4}{16}\ \frac{5}{20}\ \frac{6}{24}$
3. $\frac{1}{5} = \cancel{\frac{2}{6}}\ \frac{2}{10}\ \frac{3}{15}\ \frac{4}{20}\ \frac{5}{25}$　　4. $\frac{2}{3} = \frac{4}{6}\ \frac{6}{9}\ \cancel{\frac{8}{16}}\ \frac{10}{15}\ \frac{12}{18}$
5. $\frac{3}{12}$　　6. $\frac{2}{3}$　　7. $\frac{10}{16}$　　8. $\frac{9}{12}$　　9. $\frac{1}{6}$　　10. $\frac{6}{9}$

Page 140
1. $\frac{1}{6}$　　2. 1　　3. $\frac{1}{8}$　　4. $\frac{24}{12}$ or 2
5. 1　　6. $\frac{11}{8}$ or $1\frac{3}{8}$　　7. 1　　8. $\frac{9}{7}$ or $1\frac{2}{7}$
9. $\frac{3}{5}$　　10. $\frac{10}{9}$ or $1\frac{1}{9}$　　11. $\frac{1}{2}$　　12. $\frac{17}{13}$ or $1\frac{4}{13}$

Page 141
1. 2 out of 11, or $\frac{2}{11}$　　2. 1 out of 11, or $\frac{1}{11}$
3. 3 out of 11, or $\frac{3}{11}$　　4. 0 out of 11, or $\frac{0}{11}$
5. 5 out of 11, or $\frac{5}{11}$　　6. yellow

Page 142
1. less likely　　2. more likely
3. impossible　　4. less likely
5. certain　　6. 10 out of 24, or $\frac{10}{24}$
7. 2 out of 24, or $\frac{2}{24}$　　8. 4 out of 24, or $\frac{4}{24}$
9. 8 out of 24, or $\frac{8}{24}$　　10. a sneaker
11. a dress shoe

Page 143
1. 81　　2. 13　　3. 7　　4. 6 whales
5. 10 whales　　6. Friday　　7. 4 more whales

Page 144

6. (1, 5)　　7. (5, 3)　　8. (4, 5)　　9. (3, 3)
10. (1, 2)　　11. (4, 1)

Page 145

A. (3,3)　　B. (-2,1)　　C. (2,-3)
D. (-3,-3)　　E. (-4,3)　　F. (4,-2)

Page 146
1.　　2.　　3.
4.　　5.　　6.
7.　　8.　　9.
10.　　11.　　12.

Page 147
1. equilateral　　2. isosceles　　3. scalene
4. scalene　　5. scalene　　6. equilateral
1. right　　2. obtuse　　3. acute
4. obtuse　　5. right　　6. acute

Page 148
1. 4:15
2. 698 bundles
3. Scott—250 papers; Monica—875 papers; Paige and her brother—3,000 papers; Eric—125 papers; total—4,250 newspapers
4. $1,889.30
5. 322 yards
6. 510 sq. mi.
7. $34.00

Page 149
1. $14.83　　2. $5.75　　3. 26,000 ml, yes
4. $32.00　　5. $20.25　　6. $4.67

Page 150
1. $12.90　　2. 6:45　　3. $59.50
4. $1.46　　5. 42 pages, 1 card
6. $14.77　　7. $4.93　　8. $8.33